Hamlet

A Study Guide for

WJEC Eduqas A-Level English Literature

Izzy Ingram

Notable

www.notableguides.co.uk

Notable

www.notableguides.co.uk

Notable is a brand new company, producing textbooks and study guides for the new A-Level courses. Whilst other textbooks give you a general overview of a topic or subject, our guides are tailored to meet the specific requirements of your exam board, so that you know exactly what to do in order to achieve the very best grade possible.

For revision tips and tricks, and to have your say on what guide we write next, follow us on social media:

Follow us on Facebook

@notableguides

Follow us on Instagram

@notable_guides

Contents

What to expect from this guide

This guide has been written for A-Level students studying English Literature with WJEC Eduqas. For this qualification, you have three different papers to sit: Poetry (Component 1), Drama (Component 2) and the Unseen (Component 3). Component 4 is a coursework essay (non-exam assessment).

This guide has been written for section A on the Component 2: Drama paper. This section is based on the study of one Shakespeare play. There are a number of Shakespearean plays to choose from, but this guide has been written to accommodate students studying *Hamlet*. The exam board do not specify a required edition, so centres are free to select any edition of the play that they wish.

Some key points to bear in mind for this paper:

- This is a **closed-book** examination. You will <u>not</u> have copies of the play with you whilst you sit the exam. Therefore, it is vital that you learn some key quotations.

- You will answer **two questions** in this section of the paper: part (i) and part (ii).

- For **part (i)**, you will be given an extract from the play. You will have to write a short essay in response to a question based on this extract.

- **Part (ii)** will ask a question concerning the entire play. Candidates must write an essay in response to the question, which analyses the play as a whole and its context.

- Altogether, the exam lasts for two hours, and you have **one hour** for this half of the paper. If you decide to do this half of the paper first, you must ensure that you do not overrun, and that you leave one hour for Section B, since this is also worth 60 marks. Equally, if you decide to begin with Section B, it is important that you leave enough time to complete Section A fully.

Synopsis

Before approaching this guide, students are expected to have read through *Hamlet* thoroughly. Nevertheless, this synopsis is here to refresh your memory:

The play is set in Elsinore, Denmark. At midnight, on the battlements of Elsinore castle, Marcellus and Barnado take Horatio to see a Ghost, which they have now spotted on two occasions. The Ghost appears again; Horatio sees it and attempts to talk to it, but it says nothing and departs.

The Danish king ("Old Hamlet") has just died, and he has been succeeded by his brother, Claudius. Claudius has married Gertrude, his brother's widow. Hamlet, the son of Gertrude and the recently deceased king, refuses to celebrate their wedding. He wears black and stands apart, mournful and downcast.

Claudius tells the court that Fortinbras, the prince of Norway, is laying claim to land that his father ("Old Fortinbras"), who is now dead, once forfeited to Old Hamlet. Claudius sends ambassadors to Norway to deal with this threat.

Laertes asks Claudius' permission to return to France, where he is studying. Laertes is the son of

Polonius, a counsellor to the king. Claudius grants him permission, and, before he leaves, Laertes warns his sister, Ophelia, to be wary of Prince Hamlet. He has noticed that Hamlet has affection for Ophelia, and has wanted to spend time alone with her. Polonius then reinforces this message, ordering his daughter to stay away from the prince.

Horatio takes Hamlet to see the Ghost. The Ghost beckons to Hamlet, and the prince talks to it, alone. It tells him that it is the Ghost of his dead father, and that he was murdered by Claudius, his brother. The Ghost asks Hamlet to avenge him by murdering his uncle. Hamlet agrees to perform this task, and he decides to pretend to be mad to avoid suspicion.

Ophelia has been evading Hamlet, as she was ordered to do. She tells Polonius, in distress, that Hamlet has been behaving like a mad man. Polonius believes that this has occurred out of love for Ophelia. Claudius and Gertrude are becoming increasingly worried about Hamlet's behaviour, and so they ask Rosencrantz and Guildenstern, old school friends of Hamlet's, to discover the cause behind his recent behaviour.

The ambassadors sent to Norway return with the news that Fortinbras' uncle is going to prevent his nephew from sending an army against Denmark. Polonius tells the King and Queen that Hamlet's madness has been caused by his love for Ophelia. In order to check that this is true, they plan to have Ophelia talk to the prince whilst Polonius and Claudius spy on their conversation. Hamlet speaks to Ophelia rudely and tells her that he never loved her.

Hamlet plans to arrange a play in which a murder similar to that committed by Claudius will be performed. He hopes that this will reveal Claudius' guilt, thereby confirming the fact that the Ghost is truly the spirit of his dead father, and not an evil spirit. The play is performed: the actor playing the king falls asleep, and his murderer pours poison in his ear, just as Claudius did. Claudius rises from his seat and leaves the room.

Gertrude asks Rosencrantz and Guildenstern to send Hamlet to her room. Polonius tells Claudius that he will spy on the queen and the prince.

On his way to his mother's room, Hamlet comes across Claudius. The king is attempting to pray, but he cannot do so properly because he will not give up the rewards that his crime won for him: his throne and his wife. Hamlet assumes that the king is confessing his sins and being forgiven, and so he refuses to kill him, since he fears that Claudius will go to heaven, having been redeemed.

Hamlet reprimands his mother for her marriage to Claudius. He then hears movement behind

9

the arras, and, thinking that Claudius is behind it, he rashly stabs it. However, it was, in fact, Polonius that was hidden there, and thus the king's counsellor dies. Hamlet continues to speak aggressively with his mother, and the Ghost enters the stage again, though the queen cannot see it. It reprimands Hamlet for delaying the task of vengeance for so long. Hamlet assures his mother that he is not truly mad, and instructs her to stop sleeping with Claudius.

Gertrude reports the news of Polonius' death to Claudius. Rosencrantz and Guildenstern are sent to England with letters arranging Hamlet's death. Hamlet comes across some of Fortinbras' soldiers, who are marching to Poland. Faced with this impressive sight, Hamlet scolds himself for continuing to delay his revenge.

On hearing the news of her father's death, Ophelia has lost her mind. This news also reaches Laertes and, enraged, he returns to Denmark to confront the king. Claudius convinces him that Hamlet, his father's murderer, is their common enemy, and they plot to kill the prince. They arrange a fencing match between Hamlet and Laertes; Laertes' blade will be poisoned. Claudius will also poison a goblet of wine, and hand it to Hamlet as refreshment. Gertrude then reports that Ophelia has drowned.

Two grave diggers prepare Ophelia's grave. Hamlet and Horatio enter the graveyard, and the prince meditates on the inevitability of death. The funeral procession arrives, and Hamlet and Laertes fight over the grave. After this, Hamlet tells Horatio that he discovered Claudius' plan to have him killed in England, and so he wrote a new letter, pretending to be Claudius, which instructed the English king to execute Rosencrantz and Guildenstern instead.

The fencing match between Laertes and Hamlet commences. Hamlet scores the first two hits, and Gertrude celebrates this by drinking the poisoned wine. Laertes wounds Hamlet with the poisoned blade; however, Laertes himself is also cut by the blade, and thus he too is poisoned. Gertrude, whilst dying, warns Hamlet that the goblet is poisoned. Hamlet wounds Claudius with the poisoned blade and forces him to drink the poisoned wine. Claudius dies. Laertes and Hamlet forgive each other, and then Laertes dies as well.

Fortinbras' army is heard returning from Poland. Hamlet appoints Fortinbras the next king of Denmark, and then dies. Fortinbras promises to hear a full account of the events that have taken place from Horatio, and instructs his men to carry Hamlet's body away in a manner befitting a soldier.

Part (i)

Format

This part of the exam paper is all about close reading. You will be given an extract from the play, and asked a question about it; for example:

Polonius: What is't, Ophelia, he hath said to you?

Ophelia: So please you, something touching the Lord Hamlet.

Polonius: Marry well bethought.
'Tis told me, he hath very oft of late
Given private time to you; and you yourself
Have of your audience been most free and bounteous.
If it be so, as so 'tis put me,
And that in way of caution, I must tell you,
You do not understand yourself so clearly
As it behoves my daughter and your honour.
What is between you? Give me up the truth.

Ophelia: He hath, my lord, of late made many tenders
Of his affection to me.

Polonius: Affection! Pooh, you speak like a green girl,
Unsifted in such perilous circumstance.
Do you believe his tenders, as you call them?

Ophelia: I do not know, my lord, what I should think.

King: Marry, I'll teach you; think yourself a baby;
That you have ta'en these tenders for true pay,
Which are not sterling. Tender yourself more dearly;
Or – not to crack the wind of the poor phrase,
Running it thus – you'll tender me a fool.

Ophelia: My lord, he hath importuned me with love
In honourable fashion.

Polonius: Ay, fashion you may call it; go to, go to.

Act I scene iii

(i) With close reference to the language and imagery in
this passage, examine how Shakespeare presents Polonius'
relationship with his daughter. [15]

The passage will always be roughly of this length. You
have **twenty minutes** to answer the question. This is not
very long, and therefore the examiners are not
expecting you to write a particularly lengthy answer.
One and a half to two sides of paper should suffice.
There is no need to worry about an introduction or a
conclusion, either. Though it is a good idea to begin
your essay with an introductory sentence, you simply do

not have the time for a full introductory paragraph. Instead, launch straight into your analysis of the passage.

Notice that there are **fifteen marks** available for this question. Five of these are for AO1, whilst the remaining ten are for AO2. No other assessment objective is credited for this part of the paper. This means that you will **not** gain marks for quoting critics, discussing the context or the play, or drawing connections between the passage and other works of literature. Instead, try to stay keenly focussed on the passage that you have been given. Though it is acceptable to make a small reference to another part of the play if it is strictly relevant and useful for your analysis, the bulk of your answer must examine the passage that you have been given.

To reiterate: **the only assessment objectives that you need to consider for the passage-based question are AO1 and AO2.** The table on page 15 provides further information on these. *The text in italics comes directly from the WJEC Eduqas specification.*

AO1	5 marks	*Articulate, informed, personal and creative responses to literary texts, using associated terminology and coherent, accurate, written expression.* In order to gain AO1 marks for this question, you must organise your essay sensibly and coherently. You must use terminology (such as similes or personification, for example) when it is relevant and helpful to do so. You must also write in a sophisticated and academic style.
AO2	10 marks	*Analyse ways in which meanngs are shaped in literary texts.* AO2 is traditional literary analysis. You must pick out important quotations from the text and analyse them, evaluating Shakespeare's use of language and dramatic techniques. If there are implicit, underlying meanings in the passage, pick them out and discuss them.

Addressing AO1

In Part (i), there are **5 marks available for AO1**. AO1 is part of every component in the WJEC Eduqas English Literature course. This is because it requires candidates to <u>write well</u>, and, in any essay, regardless of the subject matter, it is essential that you do this. That said, it is difficult to 'revise' for this assessment objective. Reading for pleasure, however, will help to improve your writing style. Moreover, this section will outline some of the criteria which is required for a good AO1 mark, and provide a few tips on how to ensure that your writing is sophisticated and formal in tone.

<u>An Academic Register:</u>

For a good AO1 mark, candidates are expected to adopt a *"clear academic style and register"*. Clearly, this means that you must avoid colloquial and informal terms. Here are some other points to bear in mind:

1) <u>Avoid using the first person pronoun</u>. Phrases such as "I think…" or "In my opinion…" establish a personal tone. In order to adopt an "academic register", you must be objective and analytical.

2) <u>Refer to the play as a play</u>. This may seem like an obvious point, but many candidates use phrases such as "in the book" or terms such as "narrative" or "the reader". It is always important to bear in mind that Shakespeare was envisaging the performance of his work as he wrote; he did not intend for his material to be read.

3) <u>Avoid contractions</u>, such as "wouldn't", "can't" or "shouldn't". Instead, write "would not", "cannot" or "should not".

4) Plays should always be referred to *in italics*. If you write by hand in examinations, you can indicate this by underlining the titles of the plays, like so: <u>Hamlet.</u>

5) When you are referring to a technique used by a playwright, make sure that you are writing in the <u>present tense</u>. For example, write "Shakespeare **employs** imagery of disease and pollution throughout the play", rather than "Shakespeare employed imagery of disease and pollution…"

Spelling, Grammar and Punctuation:

It is important that you avoid making spelling, punctuation and grammatical errors which might irritate an English Literature examiner. Of course, this is easier said than done when you are writing under examination conditions. This is why time management is so crucial; try to leave yourself two minutes at the end of the exam to read over your essay and ensure that you fix any accidental mistakes.

Terminology:

Meeting AO1 also involves using literary terminology. This means that you must make references to the **similes, metaphors, personification** et cetera which are being employed by the playwright to achieve a certain effect. However, it is vital that you use these terms relevantly, assessing their purpose and effect. English literature examiners are always frustrated by "labelling". This is when you identify a simile, for example, but do not analyse its effect. Identifying literary terms for its own sake will never gain you any credit at A-level. Similarly, it is important that you do not 'overuse' terminology. Whilst it can help you to make your analysis more specific, it should be used sparingly and thoughtfully.

Organisation:

There are also AO1 marks available for organising your essay effectively and sensibly.

Of course, part (i) only requires candidates to write a short answer in response to the passage, consisting of two or three paragraphs. It is easy, as a result, to fall into the trap of simply writing down all your thoughts and annotations of the passage, without attempting to structure them. To avoid this, it is a good idea to jot down at least two main points that come to mind, in response to the question. Your first paragraph will be based on point 1, and your second on point 2. Then, gather evidence and quotations from the passage to support those points. Doing this will ensure that your answer, though short, still shows evidence of structure and organisation. We will go over some tips on organising your response in more detail in the "Approaching a Question" section on page 22.

It is also important to bear in mind that you are **not** expected to write an introduction or a conclusion for this answer; you simply do not have the time. However, in order to make sure your answer has a good structure, it is a good idea to open with an introductory sentence. This will probably look something like this:

In this extract, in which Hamlet informs Horatio of the deaths of Rosencrantz and Guildenstern, before declaring his intention to avenge his father, Shakespeare presents his protagonist as a changed hero who is now capable of taking decisive action.

You should never waste too much time describing what happens in a passage (you are not re-telling the story, but analysing the text). However, it is a good idea to begin your answer with a brief comment like the one above, which shows that you understand what is occurring, before quickly moving onto your argument, which, in this case, is that "Shakespeare presents his protagonist as a changed hero who is now capable of taking action".

Addressing AO2

AO2 is literary analysis, and it is included in every paper of your English Literature A-Level. For Part (i), this is worth **10 marks**. You should be focussing closely on the passage, pulling out key quotations and images, and showing how they support your response to the question. You must be using quotations from the extract to support your answer; the exam board states that "confident and apt textual support" is required for the highest AO2 marks.

In addition, the exam board requires candidates to demonstrate "perceptive, sophisticated analysis and evaluation of Shakespeare's use of language and dramatic techniques to create meaning." So, if the passage contains "dramatic techniques", such as exits or entrances, you will gain credit for analysing these, as well as the **dialogue**.

There is clearly some overlap with AO1 here: if you are writing fluently, your analysis will be clearer and appear more sophisticated. Remember to be aware of 'labelling' when it comes to using literary and dramatic terminology: the exam board specifically states that you must demonstrate how Shakespeare uses techniques "to create meaning". You must assess the effect of techniques, rather than simply identifying them.

Approaching a Question

You have **twenty minutes** to answer this question. Though this is not a lot of time, it is important that you do not rush and start writing too early. Silly mistakes happen in exams; to minimise your chances of making them, read and reread both the passage and the question very carefully. Circle or underline key words in the question, to make sure you know exactly what is being asked of you.

Attempting practice questions under timed conditions will give you an idea of how quickly you can plan and write (there are some practice questions on page 31). Roughly, however, we would recommend spending five minutes annotating the passage, like so:

Polonius: What is't, Ophelia, he hath said to you?

Ophelia: So please you, something touching the Lord Hamlet.

Near-blasphemous phrase – angry, demanding, intimidating

Responds immediately and honestly – compliant, deferential, dutiful

Polonius: Marry well bethought.
'Tis told me, he hath very oft of late
Given private time to you; and you yourself
Have of your audience been most free and bounteous.
If it be so, as so 'tis put me,
And that in way of caution, I must tell you,

Ophelia's responses are much shorter than Polonius' – meek, passive, obedient. Their relationship is clearly an unequal one

You do not understand yourself so clearly
As it behoves my daughter and your honour.
What is between you? Give me up the truth.

Ophelia: He hath, my lord, of late made many tenders
Of his affection to me.

Imperative verbs – intrusive, demanding

Polonius: Affection! Pooh, you speak like a green girl,
Unsifted in such perilous circumstance.
Do you believe his tenders, as you call them?

Respectful, obedient

Ophelia: I do not know, my lord, what I should think.

King: Marry, I'll teach you; think yourself a baby;
That you have ta'en these tenders for true pay,
Which are not sterling. Tender yourself more dearly;
Or – not to crack the wind of the poor phrase.
Running it thus – you'll tender me a fool.

A pun which subverts Ophelia's term "tenders of affection" into a financial metaphor – scornful, ridiculing her feelings

Lexical field of transaction and bargaining – suggests that Polonius views his daughter as a commodity

Ophelia: My lord, he hath importuned me with love
In honourable fashion.

Polonius: Ay, fashion you may call it; go to, go to.

Act I scene iii

23

(i) With close reference to the language and imagery of this passage, examine how Shakespeare presents Polonius' relationship with his daughter. [15]

Annotating the passage in this way will help you to start forming ideas. Circling key words or phrases also ensures that your analysis is focussed and specific. The highest AO2 marks are awarded to candidates who 'pick apart' and tightly analyse images and phrases in this way, rather than making vague, general analytical points about the passage as a whole.

Once you have annotated the passage, it is important to organise your annotations. Remember that AO1 marks are awarded for evidence of organisation and structure. It is important, therefore, that you organise your annotations into a plan for two or three paragraphs, like so:

Paragraph (1): Polonius' treatment of Ophelia:

- Imperative verbs ('give', 'think', 'tender'), coupled with near-blasphemous phrases ('Marry well bethought') – present Polonius as aggressive and demanding.
- This contrasts with the articulate advice he gave Laertes, his son, directly before this interchange with Ophelia – suggests that he is perhaps more

- suspicious of, and certainly less respectful towards, his daughter.
- He is scornful and dismissive of her feelings: he subverts her term "tenders of affection" into a financial metaphor ("tenders for true pay which are not sterling").
- This lexical field of commerce and transaction persists throughout the passage, which perhaps serves to suggest that Polonius views Ophelia herself as a commodity, which can be bought and sold ("tender yourself more dearly").

Paragraph (2): Ophelia's attitude towards Polonius:

- Respectful: she repeatedly refers to him as "my lord".
- Obedient: she responds immediately and honestly to his question ("so please you, something touching the lord Hamlet").
- Passive: she expresses herself in short, monosyllabic sentences. Indeed, her dialogue is notably shorter than her father's. When she does speak, her remarks are cautious and non-committed ("I do not know my lord what I should think"), suggesting meekness and humility in the presence of her father.

- This suggests that their relationship is an unequal one, in which Ophelia is restricted from freely expressing herself.

This plan is good because it answers the question: both paragraphs analyse the presentation of the relationship between Ophelia and Polonius in this passage. Nonetheless, they are also different from each other: paragraph one looks at this relationship from Polonius' perspective, whilst paragraph two considers it from Ophelia's. Your answer should always follow this rough format: two or three paragraphs, which all answer the question but focus on different ideas.

Writing a plan like this will help you to organise your ideas and prevent you from falling into the trap of analysing the passage in an unorganised, line-by-line fashion.

Writing a plan also makes it easier for you to begin writing your answer. Read the Sample Answer in the next chapter to get a rough idea of what this should look like.

Sample Answer

Below is a sample passage and question, followed by an example of a high-level answer that has been written in response to it.

King: Laertes, was your father dear to you? Or are you like the painting of a sorrow, a face without a heart?

Laertes: Why ask you this?

King: Not that I think you did not love your father;
But that I know love is begun with time,
And that I see, in passages of proof,
Time qualifies the spark and fire of it.
There lives within the very flame of love
A kind of wick or snuff that will abate it,
And nothing is at a like goodness still;
For goodness, growing to a plurisy,
Dies in his own too much. That we would do
We should do when we would, for this 'would' changes,
And hath abatements and delays as many
As there are tongues, are hands, are accidents;
And then this 'should' is like a spendthrift's sigh,
That hurts by easing. But, to the quick of th'ulcer –
Hamlet comes back, what would you undertake,

To show yourself your father's son in deed
More than in words?

Laertes: To cut his throat i'th'church.

King: No place indeed should murder sanctuarize;
Revenge should have no bounds. But, good Laertes,
Will you do this, keep close within your chamber.
Hamlet returned shall know you are come home:

Act IV scene vii

(i) With close reference to the language and imagery
of this passage, examine Shakespeare's depiction of
Claudius. [15]

In this extract, in which Claudius encourages Laertes to take
revenge for the murder of Polonius, his father, Shakespeare
makes use of sentence structure in order to present the Danish
king as calm and measured. Short, emphatic clauses – "No
place should murder santuarize; revenge should have no
bounds" – provide Claudius' dialogue with a persuasive
quality, akin to a political speech. Laertes' anger and vengeful
desires, moreover, serve to juxtapose the king's measured
tranquillity, with the former's short, rageful exclamations
serving as a contrast to Claudius' lengthy dialogue. Claudius,
therefore, is presented as being calm and clear-thinking in this
passage.

Ultimately, however, Claudius' calm rationality
serves the deceitful purpose of galvanising Laertes into

removing Hamlet, "th' ulcer", from Denmark for him. There is irony, therefore, in the question the king poses to Laertes, asking if he is merely "like the painting of a sorrow" (an insensitive simile, which suggests that Laertes' grief if only an external, superficial act), since it is Claudius, the murderer of his brother, who is ultimately hiding behind deceitful appearances. Shakespeare adds particular emphasis to the insensitivity of Claudius' manipulation here, furthermore, by having Laertes respond, presumably in grief and despair, "Why ask you this?" By having the king persist in his metaphors of "goodness, growing to a plurisy", Shakespeare presents him as having little consideration for Laertes' distress. Images relating to fire, moreover, are frequently employed – "the very flame of love", "the spark and fire" – in the hope of intensifying Laertes' own 'fire', or rage, whilst the inclusive pronoun "we" is repeatedly used to stress the idea that the King and Laertes are allies, combatting a common enemy. The culmination of all these manipulative techniques is Laertes' irreligious declaration that he will "cut" Hamlet's throat "i'th'church". By encouraging this sacrilegious rage, rather than dissuading it, Shakespeare suggests that there is little that Claudius will not do in order to maintain his throne.

Good Points:

This answer is of a high standard because it is focussed, organised, and analytical. It is written in a fluent, academic style, and it focusses on the presentation of Claudius throughout (which is what the question demands) rather than simply analysing the passage. The two-paragraph structure is effective, with the first paragraph focussing on the characterisation of Claudius as calm, composed and measured, and the second focussing on his capacity for deceit and manipulation.

To Improve:

The second paragraph is somewhat longer than the first; the candidate could perhaps have devoted a little more attention to their first point. Nonetheless, this is a good response.

Practice Questions

The next few pages contain some practice questions and passages. Pick a question and annotate it, as we did on page 22. Then, write a brief plan which organises your annotations, similar to that on page 24.

Finally, try using your plan to write a full answer. Once you have done this a couple of times, repeat the process under timed conditions.

Practice Question 1:

Hamlet: Alas, poor ghost!

Ghost: Pity me not, but lend thy serious hearing
To what I shall unfold.

Hamlet: Speak; I am bound to hear.

Ghost: So art thou to revenge, when thou shalt hear.

Hamlet: What?

Ghost: I am thy father's spirit,
Doom'd for a certain time to walk the night,
And for the day confined to fast in fires,
Till the foul crimes done in my days of nature

Are burnt and purged away. But that I am forbid
To tell the secrets of my prison-house,
I could tell a tale unfold whose lightest word
Would harrow up thy soul, freeze thy young blood,
Make thy two eyes, like stars, start from their spheres,
Thy knotted and combined locks to part
And each particular hair to stand on end,
Like quills upon the fretful porpentine:
But this eternal blazon must not be
To ears of flesh and blood. List, list, O, list!
If thou didst ever thy dear father love –

Hamlet: O God!

Ghost: Revenge his foul and most unnatural murder.

Hamlet: Murder!

Ghost: Murder most foul, as in the best it is;
But this most foul, strange and unnatural.

Act 1 Scene v

(i) With close reference to the language and imagery in this
passage, examine how Shakespeare creates an atmosphere
of foreboding and fear. [15]

Practice Question 2:

King: O my offence is rank, it smells to heaven;
It hath the primal eldest curse upon't,
A brother's murder. Pray can I not,
Though inclination be as sharp as will.
My stronger guilt defeats my stronger intent,
And like a man to double business bond,
I stand in pause when I shall first begin,
And both neglect. What if this cursed hand
Were thicker than itself with brother's blood,
Is there not rain enough in the sweet heavens
To wash it white as snow? Whereto serves mercy
But to confront the visage of offence?
And what's in prayer but this two-fold force,
To be forestalled ere we come to fall,
Or pardoned being down? Then I'll look up;
My fault is past. But o what form of prayer
Can serve my turn? 'Forgive me my foul murder?'
That cannot be since I am still possessed
Of those effects for which I did the murder,
My crown, mine own ambition, and my Queen,
May one be pardoned and retain th'offence?
In the corrupted currents of this world
Offence's gilded hand may shove by justice,
And oft 'tis seen the wicked prize itself
Buys out the law. But 'tis not so above;

There is no shuffling, there the action lies
In his true nature, and we ourselves compelled,
Even to the teeth and forehead of our faults
To give in evidence. What then? What rests?
Try what repentance can – what can it not?
Yet what can it, when one can not repent?
O wretched state, o bosom black as death,
O limed soul, that struggling to be free,
Art more engaged! Help, angels, make assay.
Bow stubborn knees, and heart with strings of steel,
Be soft as sinews of the new-born babe.
All may be well.

Act III Scene iii

(i) With close reference to the language and imagery in
this passage, examine Shakespeare's depiction of
Claudius' state of mind. [15]

Practice Question 3:

Rosencrantz: What have you done my lord with the dead body?

Hamlet: Compounded it with dust whereto 'tis kin.

Rosencrantz: Tell us where 'tis that we may take it thence, and bear it to the chapel.

Hamlet: Do not believe it.

Rosencrantz: Believe what?

Hamlet: That I can keep your counsel, and not my own. Besides, to be demanded of a sponge, what replication should be made by the son of a king?

Rosencrantz: Take you me for a sponge my lord?

Hamlet: Ay sir, that soaks up the King's countenance, his rewards, his authorities. But such officers do the King best service in the end; he keeps them like an ape in the corner of his jaw, first mouthed to be last swallowed. When he needs what you have gleaned, it is but squeezing you, and sponge, you shall be dry again.

Rosencrantz: I understand you not my lord.

Hamlet: I am glad of it; a knavish speech sleeps in a foolish ear.

Rosencrantz: My lord, you must tell us where the body is, and go with us to the King.

Hamlet: The body is with the King, but the King is not with the body. The King is a thing –

Guildenstern: A thing my lord!

Hamlet: Of nothing. Bring me to him. Hide fox, and all after.

Act 4 Scene II

(i) With close reference to the language and imagery in this passage, examine Shakespeare's presentation of Hamlet. [15]

Practice Question 4:

Laertes: How now, what noise is that?

Enter OPHELIA

O heat, dry up my brains, tears seven times salt
Burn out the sense and virtue of mine eye.
By heaven, thy madness shall be paid with weight,
Till our scale turn the beam. O rose of May,
Dear maid, kind sister, sweet Ophelia –
O heavens, is't possible a young maid's wits
Should be as mortal as an old man's life?
Nature is fine in love, and where 'tis fine,
It sends some precious instance of itself
After the thing it loves.

Ophelia: [*Sings*]
      They bore him barefaced on the bier;
       Hey non nonny, nonny, hey nonny,
       And in his grave rained many a tear –
      Fare you well my dove.

Laertes: Hadst thou thy wits, and didst persuade revenge,
It could not move thus.

Ophelia: You must sing 'A-down a-down', an you call
him a-down-a. O how the wheel becomes it! It is the false
steward that stole his master's daughter.

Laertes: This nothing's more than matter.

Ophelia: There's rosemary, that's for remembrance – pray you love, remember – and there is pansies, that's for thoughts.

Laertes: a document in madness, thoughts and remembrance fitted.

Ophelia: There's fennel for you, and columbines. There's rue for you, and here's some for me; we may call it herb of grace a Sundays – o you must wear your rue with a difference. There's a daisy, I would give you some violets, but they withered all when my father died – they say 'a made a good end –
[*Sings*] For bonny sweet Robin is all my joy.

Laertes: Thought and affliction, passion, hell itself, She turns to favour and to prettiness.

Act 4 Scene V

(i) With close reference to the language and imagery in this passage, examine how Shakespeare creates pathos at this point in the play. [15]

Practice Question 5:

Guildenstern: My lord, we were sent for.

Hamlet: I will tell you why; so shall my anticipation prevent your discovery, and your secrecy to the king and queen moult no feather. I have of late, but wherefore I know not, lost all my mirth, forgone all custom of exercises; and indeed it goes so heavily with my disposition that this goodly frame the earth, seems to me a sterile promontory, this most excellent canopy, the air, look you, this brave o'erhanging firmament, this majestical roof fretted with golden fire, why, it appears no other thing to me than a foul and pestilent congregation of vapours. What a piece of work is a man, how noble in reason, how infinite in faculties, in form and moving, how express and admirable in action, how like an angel! in apprehension, how like a god; the beauty of the world, the paragon of animals. And yet, to me, what is this quintessence of dust? Man delights not me; no, nor woman neither, though by your smiling you seem to say so.

Rosencrantz: My lord, there was no such stuff in my thoughts.

Hamlet: Why did you laugh then, when I said 'man delights not me'?

Act 2 Scene ii

(i) With close reference to the language and imagery in this passage, examine Shakespeare's presentation of Hamlet's state of mind. [15]

Part (ii)

Format:

Part (ii) forms the larger part of Section A. It is worth **45 marks**. This means that you should devote roughly **40 minutes** to answering this question.

In contrast to Part (i), Part (ii) will not involve a passage. Instead, you will be asked **a general question about the entire play**. This is a closed book examination, so you will not have a copy of *Hamlet* in the exam with you. This means that you must learn some key quotations from the play.

Again unlike Part (i), Part (ii) requires you to draw contextual details (AO3) and critical material (AO5) into your answer. You must write a full essay, with an introduction and a conclusion.

The grid on pages 42 and 43 provides more information on the assessment objectives for this question. *The text in italics comes directly from the WJEC Eduqas specification.* **Note that AO3 (context) is worth more marks than any other assessment objective.**

AO1	5 marks	*Articulate, informed, personal and creative responses to literary texts, using associated concepts and terminology, and coherent, accurate written expression.*
		In essence, this assessment objective requires students to <u>write well</u>. Candidates must: - keep spelling and grammatical errors to a minimum - use relevant literary terms - use an academic register - organise your essay in a sensible and coherent way - be fully engaged with the question throughout
AO2	10 marks	*Analyse ways in which meanings are shaped in literary texts.* AO2 is traditional literary analysis. Candidates must: - refer to relevant quotations from the play - analyse the playwright's use of language - analyse the playwright's use of dramatic techniques - demonstrate an understanding of underlying meanings

AO3	20 marks	*Demonstrate an understanding of the significance and influence of the contexts in which literary texts are written and received.*
		This is exactly what the exam board say it is: you must discuss the context in which the play was written or received, and, for the highest marks, this must be relevant and serve to deepen and further your analysis.
		Look at the number of marks available: it is <u>double</u> that of any other assessment objective.
AO5	10 marks	*Explore literary texts informed by different interpretations.*
		There is never one way in which a text can be understood, and, in order to gain AO5 marks, you must show that you understand this. This can be achieved by referring to critics, referring to productions or films, applying a theory-based approach (such as Marxist or feminist criticism), or simply by discussing an argument from another angle.

Addressing AO1 and AO2

We discussed ideas on how to address AOs 1 and 2 in the part (i) section. Those ideas apply to part (ii) as well, so it's worth having a reread of those; we won't reiterate them here.

However, here are some additional tips which specifically apply to a part (ii) style question:

- For part (ii), you are required to write a much longer essay than in part (i). You have roughly **forty minutes** to complete it. You have more ideas to consider (because you are analysing the entire play, and because you are drawing AOs 3 and 5 into the discussion as well), and you must write an introduction and a conclusion. All this means that you have a lot of information to grapple with, and thus organisation is crucial. We recommend spending 5 to 10 minutes writing a brief plan. This will ensure that your essay shows evidence of structure, which will gain you AO1 marks.

- AO1 marks are available for remaining focussed on the question – so ensure that you are consistently addressing it. This is especially important in part (ii), because the question is more specific and focussed.

- You will not have a copy of the play with you in the exam. Therefore, you must memorise key quotations: AO2 marks are awarded for apt and relevant textual support.

- Whilst it is acceptable to use quotations from the passage in part (i) for your part (ii) answer, only do so if the quotation is relevant to your argument. You must also be wary of overusing quotations from the passage: remember that the examiner knows which passage has been given to you in part (i), and they will not find it impressive if you are simply regurgitating large parts of it in part (ii).

AO2 also requires candidates to evaluate underlying, or implicit, meanings. One way in which this can be achieved is by analysing **motifs** and **symbols**. This is because a symbol, by its very nature, is something which has an underlying or alternative meaning.

In *Hamlet*, physical objects are not often used to represent the key ideas or themes of the play, but there are a few important ones. Take a moment to read through the next few pages, which discuss some of these.

Yorick's Skull

If you were asked to think of an image which you associated with *Hamlet*, the first thing to come into your head would probably be a skull. It is the play's most famous symbol.

Hamlet is a play which is deeply concerned with death. The protagonist's famous "To be or not to be" soliloquy asks us why we continue to live when life involves so much hardship and suffering. Ophelia makes the choice to end her own life, whilst all the other major characters are killed over the course of the play. Human life appears fragile, painful and pointless.

When Hamlet enters the graveyard in Act V scene i, he is once again confronted with death. As he observes, human life appears to come to nothing. Whether you were Alexander the Great in life, or someone of no fame or renown, we all end up in the same condition ("returneth to dust").

Hamlet's holding of Yorick's skull is deeply symbolic; metaphorically, he is looking death in the face. He is fixated with the notion that death is inevitable, and he shows a macabre fascination with what happens to the physical body after death.

He repeatedly contrasts life and action with the dead remains ("Here hung those lips that I have kissed I know not how oft. Where be your gibes now? Your gambols, your songs, your flashes of merriment, that were wont to set the table roar?"). He is trying to understand how these things can simply come to nothing.

Some critics suggest that, after this moment, Hamlet is transformed. He is active and ready, finally, to execute revenge. Rather than philosophising and mourning life's hardships, he entrusts his fate to a supernatural power ("there is special providence in the fall of a sparrow"), and is prepared to act, regardless of the consequences. The episode with Yorick's skull, therefore, is perhaps intended to mark the moment at which Hamlet comes to terms with death after so much shock and grief, after which he is able to live his life and act as he has been commanded long ago by the Ghost.

This is one interpretation of the play, and, as with any interpretation, you do not have to agree with it. Instead, you might argue that Hamlet never comes to terms with death. You are always free to argue however you choose, so long as you can support your view with

Ophelia's Flowers

After the death of Polonius, Ophelia loses her sanity. This erodes her selfhood as well; as Claudius remarks, she is "divided from herself and her fair judgement, without the which we are pictures, or mere beasts." She sings, makes uncharacteristically bawdy comments, and distributes flowers. These flowers had special, symbolic meanings. Fennel, for example, signified flattery, whilst columbines symbolised marital infidelity. Rue traditionally signified repentance, whilst violets represented faithfulness. There are no stage directions in the original text; a director must decide who Ophelia hands these to.

You might argue that this is simply a random act, which Ophelia performs because of her madness. She is not intending to issue judgements on the other characters by handing them the flowers; if she does so, she is not conscious of it.

Alternatively, you could suggest that Ophelia is conscious of what she is doing. In fact, you could go so far as to argue that there is "method" in her madness, just as there is in that of Hamlet. Throughout the play, she has had to keep her opinions and ideas to herself, repeatedly insisting that she thinks "nothing". Now, under the guise of madness, she is able to express her opinions of the other characters, by handing them certain flowers. We'll discuss this interpretation in greater detail on page 121.

Either way, as a result of this moment in the play, Ophelia has come to be associated with flowers. In paintings, she is often depicted drowning amongst them. As Laertes points out, "Thought and affliction, passion, hell itself, she turns to favour and to prettiness." She is, perhaps, always characterised by "prettiness", regardless of the pain she suffers, and her flowers contribute towards this image.

Poison, Disease and Decay

Claudius kills his brother by pouring poison in his ear whilst he is sleeping. This, as we will discuss on page 63, is Shakespeare's invention; in his sources for the story, the old king is simply stabbed. Why do you think Shakespeare decided to make this change?

One reason might be that pouring poison into a sleeping man's ear is a far more cowardly murder method than stabbing him. Perhaps Shakespeare was simply trying to establish Claudius as a weak and cowardly individual; the king's cowardly actions later in the play could be cited as supporting evidence for this argument.

In addition, it could also be argued that Shakespeare is trying to establish poison as a motif here, which will recur throughout the play. Language and imagery relating to poison, disease and decay are everywhere in *Hamlet*. Marcellus notices that there is "something rotten in the state of Denmark"; Hamlet argues that "some vicious mole of nature", a single flaw, can destroy a man's reputation; Gertrude claims that her soul is marred with "black and grained spots". Laertes, whilst warning his sister to be wary of Hamlet's advances, tells her that the "canker galls the infants of the spring too oft before their buttons be disclosed". "For if the sun breed maggots in a dead dog, being a god kissing carrion", remarks Hamlet, as he mocks Polonius. One could very easily go on.

The point of such images is perhaps to emphasise the fact that Claudius' initial poison – that which he poured in his brother's ear – has, metaphorically, 'spread' throughout the nation, corrupting it. This idea is influenced by the medieval theory of microcosm and macrocosm, which was still influential in Shakespeare's time. This theory claimed that a monarch's physical and emotional state was representative of the country as a whole; the king was the metaphorical 'head' of the state's 'body'. If there was something wrong with the 'head' (such as the king being sick or weak – or corrupt, in Claudius' case), then the 'body' would suffer too. Denmark, therefore, is 'diseased' because it's king is corrupt, and consequently images of poison and decay abound everywhere.

Addressing AO3

AO3 requires students to use their contextual knowledge in order to enhance their analysis of the play. It is the <u>most important assessment objective</u> in this paper, because it is worth 20 marks. The other assessment objectives are worth 10 marks, with the exception of AO1, which is worth only 5 marks (see grid on pages 42 and 43). It is crucial, therefore, that you are consistently embedding contextual information into your answer, and using it to further your argument.

In order to achieve high marks for this assessment objective, you must not only refer to context but refer to it in a <u>relevant</u> manner. The lowest AO3 marks (1-2 out of 10) are given to students who merely "describe" the wider context, whilst the highest marks are awarded to candidates who are "productive" in their use of contextual information. This means that you must use context to further your analysis; it should not be an irrelevant sentence which is thrown into a paragraph in order to 'tick the AO3 box'.

Have a look at the difference between candidates A and B:

Candidate A: Niccolo Machiavelli was an Italian diplomat and philosopher. He lived before Shakespeare's time, but Shakespeare had probably heard of his work *The Prince*, even though it was banned in England. In this Machiavelli argues that it is acceptable to employ some "criminal or nefarious method" to achieve goals which are good for the country as a whole.

Candidate B: The ideas of Niccolo Machiavelli, an Italian political theorist, may have influenced a contemporary audience's opinion of Claudius. In his work *The Prince*, Machiavelli argues that it is acceptable to employ some "criminal or nefarious method" to achieve goals which are good for the country as a whole. Similarly, Claudius rises to power by committing a criminal and sinful act – the murder of his brother – but this is arguably for the greater good of the people, because he proves to be an articulate, diplomatic and effective ruler.

Both candidates will gain <u>some</u> AO3 credit, but candidate B's mark will be much higher, because the contextual information is relevant and useful. Candidate

B has used this information to further their literary analysis, whilst Candidate's A work could be mistaken for an extract from a history essay.

It is vital that your work remains a literary essay. This is the danger with AO3: though it is crucial that you address it, you must ensure that you do not digress from the play too much.

Revising Context:

Contextual information is one of those things which you simply have to learn. You can ensure that you use it relevantly by always relating it to the play and how it might impact our – or the original audience's – interpretation of it. This guide will help with this by drawing relevant context into discussions of key themes (see page 90 onwards).

Nevertheless, it is important to have some of the basic context 'under your belt' before we can take the discussion further: take a moment to read through the next few pages.

1) Revenge Tragedy:

As its name suggests, a revenge tragedy is a play in which the **protagonist** must avenge an atrocity committed by the **antagonist**. This genre was very popular in English theatres in the late 16th and early 17th centuries. They took inspiration from the Roman philosopher and playwright Seneca, and consequently they are characterised by violent murders and bloody horrors.

Thomas Kyd's play, *The Spanish Tragedy* (c.1580s), is often considered the first revenge tragedy. This play has much in common with *Hamlet*: a play within a play, a vengeful ghost, madness. Akin to Hamlet, Hieronimo, the play's protagonist, contemplates suicide, whilst his wife, Isabella, is driven to suicide by grief after the death of her son, in a similar way to Ophelia, who also (it is implied) kills herself after the death of a loved one.

However, there are many ways in which *Hamlet* differs from the conventions of this genre, too. Notably, there is the characterisation of Hamlet himself. He is melancholy and idle; he laments the fact that the task of revenge has fallen upon him, and repeatedly avoids and evades it. Interestingly, the characters of Laertes and Fortinbras are more typical models for the hero of a revenge tragedy than Hamlet is: they are eager to act and avenge their dead fathers. They are **foils**: characters designed to contrast with the protagonist, so as to emphasise certain qualities in him, by way of comparison. By incorporating these more traditional characters into the play, Shakespeare is emphasising how unusual and atypical a Revenge Tragedy protagonist Hamlet is.

We will discuss this idea at greater length in the chapter on "Revenge and Hamlet's Delay", beginning on page 90, but it's important to note here because the context of the revenge tragedy as a genre is clearly central to the debate concerning whether Shakespeare is conforming to, or subverting, this genre. Kiernan Ryan takes the latter view, arguing that, in *Hamlet*, Shakespeare "deliberately sabotages the whole genre of revenge tragedy by creating a tragic protagonist who refuses, for reasons he can't fathom himself, to play the stock role in which he's been miscast by the world he happens to inhabit." Using your knowledge of the revenge tragedy as a genre and of *Hamlet* itself, to what extent do you agree?

Another common feature of revenge tragedies are corrupt states. As George Norton points out, "revenge tragedies often explore the notion of corruption both political and personal [...] the revenger often finds himself at odds with a corrupt state and has to rely on his own means to achieve revenge". This is clearly the case in *Hamlet*: the "state of Denmark" is "rotten", because Claudius, a deceitful murderer, is at its head – which leads us very nicely into our next key piece of context....

2) Machiavelli:

Niccolo Machiavelli (1469-1527) was an Italian political theorist, as well as a diplomat, philosopher and humanist. Italy was not a unified country at this time; the Republic of Florence, where he was born and worked, was one of many city-states. These states were often in conflict with each other, and power changed hands frequently and violently.

Machiavelli is most famous for *The Prince*, a work of political theory that was first printed in 1532. The work was often interpreted as immoral, and, in England, it was officially placed on a list of banned books in 1599. Despite this, copies of Machiavelli's work still circulated, and his ideas had wide currency.

The Prince contemplates what makes a good ruler, and it covers many aspects of leadership. Machiavelli argues that a successful nation requires a strong leader who can ensure the safety and prosperity of his people. Controversially, he suggests that it is acceptable to employ "some criminal or nefarious method" to achieve these aims.

"... contemporary experience shows that princes who have achieved great things have been those who have given their word lightly, who have known how to trick men with their cunning, and who, in the end, have overcome those abiding by honest principles."

Machiavelli, *The Prince*,
Penguin, trans. George Bull, p.74.

"... one must know how to colour one's actions and be a great liar and deceiver. Men are so simple, and so much creatures of circumstance, that the deceiver will always find someone ready to be deceived."

P.75

"To those seeing and hearing him, he should appear a man of compassion, a man of good faith, a man of integrity, a kind and religious man."

P. 76

As the above quotations from *The Prince* demonstrate, Machiavelli believed that a successful leader ought to maintain a good public image, even if he/she was secretly performing immoral acts. Claudius implements this: consider his speech to the court in Act I scene ii, in which he pretends to mourn his brother, for example.

Indeed, it is certainly possible to argue that Claudius is an effective ruler (and we will discuss this argument in greater detail on page 107). He handles the threat posed by Fortinbras quickly and efficiently; he is an articulate public speaker and a skilled diplomat. Though his rise to power depended upon his committing an immoral act, the murder of his brother, Machiavelli suggests that such acts are acceptable if they lead to effective leadership and the greater good of the nation. Do Machiavelli's ideas alter your view of Claudius, and the play as a whole? Do you think that a contemporary audience would have felt differently?

Using Machiavelli's ideas to assess Claudius and the concept of kingship in the play is a way to use context relevantly and usefully, rather than simply regurgitating it factually.

3) Marriage and Incest:

Throughout the play, Hamlet frequently labels the marriage between his mother and Claudius, his uncle, as "incestuous". He and the ghost are the only characters to do this, and it is interesting to consider what Shakespeare's contemporaries would have thought of this union.

A key issue here is that the Bible expresses different views on this subject. Deuteronomy, a book in the Old Testament, actively encourages a man to marry his brother's widow:

"If brothers are living together and one of them dies without a son, his widow must not marry outside the family. Her husband's brother shall take her and marry her and fulfil the duty of a brother-in-law to her."

Deuteronomy 25:5

Leviticus, meanwhile, contradicts this message:

"If a man marries his brother's wife, it is an act of impurity; he has dishonoured his brother. They will be childless."

Leviticus 20:21

In 1509, Henry VIII was crowned king. Two months after his coronation, he married Catherine of Aragon. Catherine had been the wife of Henry's older brother, Arthur, who had died at the age of fifteen. Marrying one's brother's widow was against canon law, so the Pope's permission was sought and given before Henry and Catherine married. When Catherine failed to produce a male heir, however, Henry attempted to have his marriage to her annulled, arguing that it contravened the Bible. In the 1530s, he separated the Church of England from Rome and the Pope. His marriage to Catherine of Aragon was annulled, and he married Anne Boleyn. Anne gave birth to Elizabeth I, who was the ruling monarch for most of Shakespeare's life. Elizabeth owed the legitimacy of her rule to the idea that her father had been wrong to marry Catherine of Aragon, his brother's widow.

Nevertheless, *Hamlet* is not explicit on whether the marriage between Claudius and Gertrude is morally wrong. As we mentioned earlier, Hamlet and the Ghost are the only characters in the play to describe it as incestuous. Is there any evidence to suggest that the other characters consider their relationship in this way? How do you think a contemporary audience would have responded to the marriage between the Danish king and queen?

4) The End of the Century:

Scholars are not sure exactly when *Hamlet* was written. Some new research appeared in 2016 suggesting that it was probably between 1601 and 1603, though we cannot be certain. For this reason, it is most prudent, in an exam, to write that the play was written 'c.1602'.

The 'c' here stands for 'circa', the Latin word for 'around'. This means that the play was written approximately at this time.

We do know, however, that *Hamlet* was written at the mid-point of Shakespeare's career as a playwright, at the turn of the century. Naturally, at the beginning of a new century, there are concerns and anxieties about the future, and in Shakespeare's day this fear was exacerbated by the fact that Queen Elizabeth I was dying, after forty-two years on the throne. Her heir, James I, was the son of Mary Queen of Scots, who had been executed by Elizabeth in 1587. This, therefore, was a time of great change, and of venturing into the unknown.

It is perhaps for this reason that *Hamlet* poses questions concerning what makes a good king or a good court. It is philosophical; it asks us why we act, why we live, and why we do anything at all. It is interesting to link these questions to the **zeitgeist** of the time, when people were naturally contemplative in the face of a new century, a new era and a new monarch.

5) Source Material:

Most of Shakespeare's plays have identifiable sources, and examining them allows us an insight into his creative choices, by revealing the changes and alterations that he decided to make.

In his *Historiae Danicae*, Danish historian Saxo Grammaticus tells a story inspired by Norse legends. In this, the king of Jutland, Horwendil, is murdered by his brother, Fengo, who then marries his widow, Gerutha. Horwendil's son, Amleth, then has to avenge his father, and pretends to be mad in order to achieve this task.

Three hundred years later, in the sixteenth century, this story was read and re-told by François de Belleforest, a French author and translator. Belleforest doubled the length of the original story, however, and made certain changes. In Belleforest's account, as in Shakespeare's, a courtier spying for Fengo is killed whilst hiding behind a tapestry.

Interestingly, in the 1580s, a play resembling *Hamlet* was performed, which has now been lost. Scholars refer to this earlier version of the play as the *Ur*-Hamlet. Whilst some critics argue that the *Ur*-Hamlet was written by Shakespeare himself (a kind of 'first attempt'), most scholars argue that the play was produced too early to belong to Shakespeare, and have suggested other playwrights, such as Thomas Kyd, author of *The Spanish Tragedy*.

Examining these sources provides us with an insight into the material which Shakespeare decided to keep, change or reject. Claudius' decision to murder his brother through the pouring of poison in his ear, for example, appears to be an alteration made by Shakespeare; in Saxo and Belleforest's accounts, Fengo simply stabs his brother. Moreover, neither Fortinbras nor Laertes appear in Saxo or Belleforest's versions of the story, which suggests that they are Shakespeare's own creations. As we discussed in the section on the revenge tragedy (page 53), these characters are used by Shakespeare as foils to Hamlet. This comparison serves to emphasise how unusual Hamlet is; his melancholy and procrastination are not typical for the hero of a revenge tragedy. Does this suggest that Shakespeare deliberately altered his sources to make them suitable for making a subversive attack on the revenge tragedy as a genre?

6) Aristotle's *Poetics*

Aristotle was an Ancient Greek philosopher, who lived in the 4th century BCE. Along with his tutor Plato, he is often considered the father of Western philosophy. His writings cover a vast range of subjects, from physics to politics, zoology to literature. His *Poetics* (c. 335 BCE) is the earliest surviving work in the Western world on dramatic theory.

For this reason, a discussion of this work will always serve as useful contextual information in an analysis of any play. However, it is important to bear in mind that the *Poetics* was lost to European society for a long time (during the Renaissance, the text was only available through a Latin translation of an Arabic translation). This means that it is very unlikely that Shakespeare was aware of Aristotle's work. Therefore, it is important that you are careful when you use Aristotelian concepts in connection with Shakespeare. Though you can (and should!) refer to his ideas and terminology, make it clear that you understand that Shakespeare was not using them consciously.

According to Aristotle, the purpose of tragedy is **catharsis**. It causes us to feel pity and fear, which then purges us of these emotions, allowing spectators to leave the theatre and live their lives with a more moderate and healthy temperament. Tragedy, therefore, has a kind of purifying or cleansing effect.

Aristotle also argues that the plot ("mythos") of a tragedy involves a "**peripeteia**", meaning a "reversal of fortune". The best kind of peripeteia involves an "**anagnorisis**" – a moment of realisation. A famous anagnorisis occurs in Sophocles' famous tragedy, *Oedipus the King*, when the **protagonist**, Oedipus, realises that he has killed his father and married his mother. Does *Hamlet* conform to this model? Is there a sudden reversal of fortune (peripeteia) or a moment of realisation (anagnorisis)?

The *Poetics* also studies the nature and defining features of the tragic hero. According to Aristotle, tragic heroes must be significant people, such as royalty. Moreover, they must not be morally reprehensible people, guilty of "vice or depravity". Instead, they must be essentially good. They must not cause tragedy by committing any kind of act of evil, but through an error of judgement. This error occurs because they have a fatal flaw, which Aristotle refers to as a "**hamartia**". In Greek Tragedy, this hamartia is often, but not always, hubris – excessive pride or arrogance, which often causes characters to treat the gods with foolish, and fatal, disrespect.

Does Hamlet have a hamartia? If so, what is it? Is he essentially good, like Aristotle suggests a tragic hero should be? His killing of Rosencrantz and Guildenstern, his treatment of Ophelia, and his manner towards Polonius' body after he has mistakenly murdered him, might all be used to suggest that Shakespeare's protagonist is in fact guilty of the "vice and depravity" that Aristotle suggests that no tragic hero should be guilty of. This, in turn, poses further questions regarding whether it is right to view Hamlet as a hero at all.

7) Ghosts, Demons and Evil Spirits

Ghosts often appear in revenge tragedy. The Roman dramatist Seneca, who, as we mentioned, inspired many Elizabethan and Jacobean playwrights, opens his *Agamemnon* with the Ghost of Thyestes attempting to incite his son to avenge the wrongs committed against him. Moreover, Kyd's *Spanish Tragedy*, which is often considered the first revenge tragedy, also involves a Ghost encouraging the living to pursue vengeance on its behalf.

However, it is important to remember that the majority of Shakespeare's contemporaries and audience members would not have considered ghosts to be, merely, a frightening but exciting trope of this genre. Rather, they were believed in and considered a real threat and genuine danger. Indeed, King James VI of Scotland, later James I of England and Ireland, published his *Daemonologie* in 1597. This work studies evil spirits and the methods they employ to corrupt human souls, showing that the king believed in and feared sorcery and witchcraft.

Protestants and Catholics differed in their beliefs on ghosts. Protestants considered them to be dangerous and evil spirits, which sought to capture and corrupt the souls of the living. Catholics, meanwhile, believed it possible that ghosts were the returned souls of the dead, delivering messages to the living. This difference arose because Catholics believed in Purgatory: a place, neither heaven nor hell, to which the dead are sent to suffer for their unconfessed sins before being allowed to enter heaven. Catholics, therefore, believed that those suffering in Purgatory could return to Earth as ghosts. Protestants, who denied the existence of Purgatory, believed that the souls of the dead could not return, and therefore ghosts were evil spirits, conjured by the devil to trick human beings.

In *Hamlet*, the Ghost heavily implies that he is suffering in Purgatory:

I am thy father's spirit,
Doomed for a certain term to walk the night,
And for the day confined to fast in fires,
Till the foul crimes done in my days of nature
Are burnt and purged away.

Act I scene v

In Shakespeare's day, however, England was a Protestant country, and the majority of Shakespeare's audience were Protestants. As we have just mentioned, Protestant theology both denied the existence of

Purgatory and the possibility of the souls of the dead returning to the land of the living.

Hamlet certainly has concerns that the Ghost may not truly be his father's spirit, but instead a "goblin damn'd", who is attempting to provoke him into committing the evil act of murder:

The spirit I have seen
May be a devil, and the devil hath power
T' assume a pleasing shape.

Act II scene ii

This context is important, because it affects our view of the protagonist. If it is possible that his father's Ghost is an evil spirit in disguise, then it poses a genuine danger. Hamlet is right to be prudent and careful, delaying the task of vengeance until he is sure (through such plots as his "Mouse-trap") that the Ghost is correct and Claudius is in fact his father's murderer. His long delay, in other words, is justified.

A. C. Bradley takes an alternative view. He argues that the Mouse-trap is not truly an act of careful evaluation and strategy. Rather, it is "an unconscious fiction, an excuse for delay – and its continuance". He suggests that Hamlet does not truly fear that the Ghost is an evil spirit; he is simply trying to delay his task for as long as possible. Which argument do you find the most convincing? Use evidence from the text to support your view.

8) Madness and Melancholia:

The theory of the four humours once formed the basis of our understanding of medicine and the human body. It dates back to Ancient Greece, and it influenced the work of figures such as Aristotle and Hippocrates. In Shakespeare's day, it remained enormously influential.

The theory argues that four fluids, known as humours, affect one's behaviour, health and personality. These four humours are blood, phlegm, black bile and yellow bile. In order to achieve good health, one must strive to keep their humours in balance. Excessive amounts of one fluid in the body can lead to dangerous and erratic behaviour, extreme emotions, and poor health.

In 1586, Timothy Bright published his *Treatise of Melancholie*. Melancholy was a malady in Elizabethan England, which, according to Bright, produced the following symptoms: "fear, sadness, desperation, tears, weeping, sobbing, sighing." It was believed to be caused by an excess of black bile in the body.

Today, we would likely categorise a condition such as this as a mental illness, resembling depression. **Be very careful when you use modern terms such as these.** Though it is perfectly acceptable to use them, make it very clear that you understand that Shakespeare would not have been aware of them, nor would his contemporary audiences. Applying modern medical terms can help you to form interesting, modern interpretations of the play – but you must ensure that you are not applying terms **anachronistically**.

It is not certain whether Shakespeare read Bright's *Treatise*, but there are some interesting parallels between *Hamlet* and this medical document. Bright writes, for example, that those afflicted by melancholy can become distracted by "fantastical apparitions". Interestingly, Hamlet is melancholic from the very outset of the play, before he meets the Ghost: he is dressed in "customary suits of solemn black", and his mother is forced to beseech him to "cast thy nighted colour off". If we apply Bright's ideas to the play, therefore, it is possible to view the Ghost as a symptom of the melancholy which Hamlet is already suffering from.

In addition to the above, Bright also writes that sufferers of the malady may have their "resolution" delayed by "long deliberation". They may also come to view their home as "a prison or dungeon, rather than a place of repose or rest". This last comment recalls Hamlet's claim, in Act II scene ii, that "Denmark's a prison".

If we entertain the idea that Shakespeare did read Bright's work (whilst making it very clear that it is by no means certain that he did) and suggest that he wants us to see Hamlet as someone who is suffering from melancholy, a disease, how does this affect our view of the protagonist, and the play as whole?

9) Kingship and Religion:

As we mentioned in our discussion of "Marriage and Incest" (page 58), Henry VIII split from the Roman Catholic Church in the 16th Century, after he failed to persuade the Pope to annul his marriage to Catherine of Aragon. In 1536, the Act of Supremacy established the King as the Head of the Church of England, instead of the Pope. He adopted the title of Defender of the Faith.

The monarch, therefore, must perform an important religious duty. As the Head of the Church of England and the Defender of the Faith, the King or Queen must promise to maintain the Church in his or her coronation oath.

Claudius, however, is a murderer. As he confesses whilst he is attempting to pray in Act III scene iii, he is unable to repent for his crime, because he will not relinquish his "crown", "ambition" or "queen" – those things which he achieved through committing it. Consequently, he is unable to pray: "words without thoughts never to heaven go." For Shakespeare's contemporaries, therefore, it may well have been deemed deeply dangerous for a monarch to be as sacrilegiously divided from God as Claudius is. This context is useful, therefore, in any discussion of Claudius' leadership qualities.

In 1599, moreover, James VI of Scotland, later James I of England and Ireland, wrote his *Basilikon Doron* (which means 'Royal Gift'). This treatise of government takes the form of a letter, addressed to James' son, Henry. The King offers his son guidance on how to be a successful and effective ruler.

In this, James I discusses a principle known as the "Divine Right of Kings". This (originally biblical) concept held that a king was not subject to any earthly authority; rather, a monarch lives and rules to serve God. Indeed, the kind is appointed by God to rule over the people. This divine appointment is what gives his rule legitimacy, and what makes him an effective ruler.

Claudius, of course, is not appointed to the throne by God. Instead, he rises to this position through his own action, by murdering his brother. He is not God's representative on earth, but a "cutpurse", who "from a shelf the precious diadem stole". This, therefore, further challenges the notion that Claudius is an effective leader and a good king.

Addressing AO5

Assessment Objective 5 requires candidates to assess the play from <u>different critical angles</u>. It expects students to understand that there is never one way in which a text can be understood. For the highest marks in this area, you should not only embed other critical viewpoints into your work, but <u>assess</u> the extent to which you regard them as valid.

<u>There are a variety of ways in which candidates can address AO5:</u>

1) Quoting a critic directly:

For example: *A. C. Bradley argues that, though Claudius "showed no cowardice" whilst in danger, "his first thought was always for himself."*

Paraphrasing is also acceptable: *A. C. Bradley suggests that Claudius is brave but selfish.*

Referring to a critic in this way is perhaps the clearest way to show an examiner that you are aware of and interested in readings of the play beyond your own. Thus, whilst learning critical quotations, on top of quotations from *Hamlet* itself, can appear a daunting task, **do not** decide to disregard this. Though there is no such thing as a perfect 'checklist' for English Literature – and you must ensure that your **allusions** to critics are made in a <u>relevant</u> manner – attempt to make at least <u>two references to critical material in your essay</u>. Always referring to critics in practice essays, furthermore, will help you to remember them.

The best way to learn critical quotations is, simply, to devote part of your revision time to reading critical material. Here are a few places to start you off if you are at a loss:

- There is, of course, a huge amount of criticism that has been written on this play. Have a browse through your school library, or your local library, for available material.

- Read the introduction to your own copy of *Hamlet*. We particularly recommend the introduction to the Arden edition of the play.

- The British Library have produced some interesting articles on *Hamlet,* which you can access for free.

Just type "The British Library Hamlet" into a search engine; it should be the first option to come up.

- The English and Media Centre's magazine (*Emagazine*) is excellent, and has produced several articles on *Hamlet*, as well as many other texts in the WJEC Eduqas English literature course. You will have to pay a subscription to access it *(if you are considering reading English at university, this subscription is definitely worthwhile anyway)*.

This guide will also refer to relevant critical quotations in discussions of key themes.

2) Theory-based approaches:

It is also possible to assess alternative readings by taking a theory-based approach. However, it is important to remember that many of these literary theories came into existence after *Hamlet* was written. It is **anachronistic**, therefore, to refer to Shakespeare as a "feminist" or a "Marxist", since feminism and Marxism did not exist when Shakespeare was writing.

It is also important to use tentative language when you refer to a theory, such as "a psychoanalytic reading *might* suggest…" (as opposed to, "a psychoanalytic reading *would* suggest…"). This is because a theory will never provide one response to a literary text; different feminist critics, for example, may come to different opinions. By referring to a theory tentatively, you are showing an examiner that you understand that this is only one way in which the theory can be applied.

Here are some theories for you to consider:

Feminist Criticism: Broadly speaking, feminism is the belief that men and women should have equal rights and opportunities. It rejects the idea that one sex is inherently superior to the other.

Feminist literary criticism approaches literature by applying the ideas and principles of feminism. A feminist critic might look at how a text has been shaped or influenced by patriarchal attitudes: for example, are the female characters being presented as objects from a male perspective? If the female characters assert their independence or rights, are they demonised or ridiculed? You might have heard of the **Madonna-Whore Complex**: this is when a writer depicts only two kinds of female character – saintly, obedient "Madonnas", or morally corrupt, licentious "Whores". Is there evidence of this in a text?

Conversely, a feminist critic might also consider whether a writer is attempting to challenge or undercut patriarchal attitudes in their work. This approach might be used to challenge the male-dominated **canon** and investigate whether female writers, who were perhaps popular in their time, have been excluded from it on account of their sex.

We will discuss the presentation of the play's female characters in greater depth on page 115, but it is worth noting here that critics have taken very different lines of argument when it comes to Shakespeare's portrayal of women in *Hamlet*. A. C. Bradley, for example, argues that Gertrude is a "very dull and shallow" character, who cares only about her own physical pleasure, "like a sheep in the sun". Marguerite Tassi, meanwhile, considers Gertrude to be a more noble character, who knowingly and willingly sacrifices herself at the end of the play in an attempt to save her son. Using evidence from the text, which interpretation do you find the more convincing?

Different opinions can also be taken on Ophelia, the play's other female character. For some, she is a naïve, modest and innocent girl. Bradley lends to weight to this idea, suggesting that "Ophelia is plainly quite young and inexperienced". Others, however, suggest that she is more psychologically complex and aware than readings such as Bradley's suggest. Elaine

Showalter, for example, notes that "feminism offered a new perspective on Ophelia's madness as protest and rebellion. For many feminist theorists, the madwoman was a heroine who rebels against gender stereotypes and the social order, at enormous cost." This notion will be considered in greater depth on page 121.

One charge that a feminist critic could level at this play is that the female characters are not as prominent or developed as their male counterparts. There are, for example, only two female characters, Ophelia and Gertrude, and neither dominate the stage: the former is timid and modest, insisting that she "think[s] nothing" and abiding by her father's will, whilst the latter speaks only 155 lines, which, as Clare Gunns notes, is fewer than any of the major characters, and approximately a mere 4% of the total lines in this play. Julie Christie, who played Gertrude in Kenneth Branagh's 1996 film production of the play, endorses this point, arguing that Gertrude "is not very well developed – none of the women in the play are. She's a passive character who never makes herself clear." Do you consider this a fair assessment?

The play comments on the sexuality of both women. Gertrude is condemned as "incestuous" by both Hamlet and the Ghost, whilst Laertes warns Ophelia of the importance of preserving her virginity ("The chariest maid is prodigal enough, if she unmask her beauty to the moon"). It is always important to bear in mind that these comments are made by characters in the play, and therefore it is possible that they do not have authorial endorsement from Shakespeare. Nevertheless, from a feminist perspective, how may we take issue with them?

Marxist Criticism: Marxist critics consider how power is gained, shared and maintained in a text. The theory examines how socio-economic conditions influence the actions, personality and behaviour of the characters, and ponders whether class struggles are at the root of the tensions between them.

Hamlet poses many questions regarding kingship, power, the relationship between the state and the people, courtliness and corruption (these will be discussed in greater detail on page 106). A Marxist reading might attract sympathy for figures such as Polonius, Rosencrantz and Guildenstern, suggesting that they exist in a world where everyone is striving for power in order to survive, and they have little choice but to do the same, by attempting to serve the king.

In addition, a Marxist critic may take a particularly critical view of Claudius and Hamlet, both of whom use the lower ranking characters in the play for their own purposes. Rosencrantz and Guildenstern,

Polonius and Ophelia, are all drawn into the struggle between protagonist and antagonist, and used by them to serve their own purposes. From this, a Marxist critic may well suggest that Hamlet and Claudius commodify those beneath them, using them as tools to achieve their own goals. Do you think that this reading is fair?

(Remember, when applying theories such as this, that – with the exception of the clowns in the graveyard – none of the characters in this play are of low or working-class status. Hamlet, Gertrude and Claudius wield more power than figures such as Horatio, Ophelia and Polonius because they are royalty, but the other characters are nonetheless upper-class).

Psychoanalytic Criticism: Founder of psychoanalysis Sigmund Freud suggested that our thoughts, actions, feelings and behaviour are informed not only by the conscious part of the mind, but also by the unconscious mind. This part of the psyche consists of repressed desires and forgotten memories.

A psychoanalytic reading of a text might choose to explore the psychology of its characters, and how this informs their actions. Hamlet is a deeply psychologically complex character, and his inability to act, despite his having "cause and will and strength and means" to do it, has long been the subject of psychoanalytic criticism.

A famous psychoanalytic reading of this play is the Oedipal reading, which applies Freud's Oedipus Complex to *Hamlet*. This concept, which Freud introduced in his *Interpretation of Dreams* (1899), suggests that infants develop a sexual desire for one parent and a sense of rivalry towards the other. Young boys, in other words, seek to take their father's place and have sexual relations with their mother. As a result, antagonism develops between father and son. The Oedipus Complex takes its name from Sophocles' tragedy *Oedipus the King*, in which Oedipus unwittingly murders his father and marries his mother.

Ernest Jones, a critic influenced by psychoanalysis and Freud's concept of the Oedipus Complex, argued in 1949 that Hamlet had a "deeper loathing" for "Claudius' incest with the Queen" than the murder of his father. Do you think that this is fair? Use evidence from the text to support your answer.

This reading of the play suggests that Hamlet is jealous of Claudius for doing what he himself has secretly wanted to do: murder his father and marry Gertrude. Jealousy over Claudius' marriage to his mother, rather than rage at Claudius' murder of his father, therefore, is, according to this theory, a greater cause of distress in Hamlet's life. The frequent comments and damning remarks that Hamlet makes about his mother's sexuality ("Let the bloat king tempt you again to bed, pinch wanton on your cheek, call you his mouse […] paddling in your neck with his damned fingers") could be used to support this line of argument.

Those who accept the Oedipal reading of the play often use it to explain Hamlet's delay. He is unable to murder Claudius, they argue, because he secretly wants to *be* Claudius. To take revenge on Claudius would be to take revenge on his unconscious mind and his own repressed desires.

Of course, Freud's Oedipus Complex, and indeed the entire field of psychoanalysis, did not exist in Shakespeare's time, and consequently many consider this reading of the play unconvincing and anachronistic. Though supporters of the theory may maintain that Oedipal feelings have always existed even if they have not been scientifically studied and consciously known – and thus they still have the potential to have influenced Shakespeare – others suggest that this reading simplifies the play and puts far too much emphasis on Hamlet's relationship with his mother. Regardless of which view you find the most convincing, it is certainly true that this reading of the play has influenced many modern productions. The "Closet Scene" (Act III scene iv), for example, in which Hamlet stabs Polonius behind the arras, is often played in a setting resembling a bedroom. There is, however, no clear indication that the scene does occur in the Queen's bedroom; we are simply told that they are in her "closet", which, at the time, simply meant a "private room". Freudian and Oedipal notions, therefore, have perhaps affected our ideas and assumptions about this play.

New Historicism: This approach considers the context in which a play was written, examining how the text reflects, or is shaped by, this context. This theory also suggests that we can learn more about the concerns of a time by reading and studying the literature that was produced during it.

In terms of *Hamlet,* therefore, we might consider contemporary notions and ideas regarding ghosts and evil spirits, the status of women, madness, or the revenge tragedy as a popular genre in the theatres of the time. Clearly, New Historicism relies on being familiar with contextual material, so have a look at the 'Addressing AO3' section for more detailed information.

3) Alternative Readings and Answering the Question:

Of course, it is possible to consider alternative readings yourself, without referring to a particular critic or theory (though explicitly naming a critic or theory will ensure that the examiner can clearly identify AO5 material in your work). For example, are Rosencrantz and Guildenstern concerned friends or untrustworthy and ambitious opportunists? Is Hamlet's madness entirely feigned, or is there evidence of genuine mental instability? Is order restored in the Danish court when Fortinbras enters the stage at the end of the play, or can we anticipate further violence and corruption? Analysing both points of view, by using evidence from the text to weigh up both sides, enables you to demonstrate an awareness of the fact that there are alternative ways in which the texts and their characters can be interpreted and understood.

In addition, there are also AO5 marks available for maintaining a focus on the question. This is because making a convincing argument, which comes to a balanced and sophisticated conclusion, requires you to look at the argument from both sides and consider alternative points of view.

Please note, however, that both answering the question and considering alternative readings yourself should be done <u>alongside referring to critics</u>, not on its own.

4) Referencing Productions and Films:

When an actor plays a role, he or she is interpreting a script. Similarly, directors must interpret a playwright's work when they stage a film or a play. Thus, it is possible to address AO5 by referencing productions and films.

Watching productions and films will also help you to learn quotations from the play, and to visualise *Hamlet* as a performance. As we mentioned in the chapter on 'Addressing AO1': the plays were written to be performed, not read – so do try and see a stage production if you can.

Of course, films are more readily available, if seeing a performance is not an option. It's always worth visiting your local library to see if there are copies of films which you could borrow. Kenneth Branagh's 1996 film, which he both directed and starred in, is particularly useful for students, because the original script is completely uncut and performed in full.

Clips from this film, as well as many others (such as those starring Laurence Olivier, David Tennant, Benedict Cumberbatch and Andrew Scott, to name a few) are also available on YouTube.

In addition, if you are unable to see full productions, reading reviews by theatre critics is a good way to learn of interesting interpretations, ideas and techniques used by directors and actors, which you could potentially discuss in an essay. *The Guardian* have several reviews on their website, if you need somewhere to start.

Here are some points and questions to consider about some productions of *Hamlet*:

- Laurence Olivier's 1948 film, which he directed and starred in, cuts the parts of Rosencrantz, Guildenstern and Fortinbras. Consequently, the action is more tightly focussed on Hamlet, his story and his mental disturbance. What do you think of this decision? Is something lost, by the cutting of these parts?

- The Almeida Theatre's 2017 production of *Hamlet*, directed by Robert Icke and starring Andrew Scott, emphasised the protagonist's vices and more villainous aspects. Following the murder of Polonius, Hamlet – whilst squeezing a bloodied cloth – is presenting as being amused by Rosencrantz and Guildenstern's terror as they ask, "What have you done my lord with the dead body?" Do you think that this interpretation is supported by the text? Does it prevent us from considering Hamlet a tragic hero?

- In Icke's production, modern technology (secret microphones, screens and cameras) are made use of. At the very beginning of the play, the Ghost is sighted on CCTV. Why do you think he does this?

- The Royal Shakespeare Company's 2008 Theatre Production of *Hamlet*, directed by Gregory Doron and starring David Tennant, depicted Gertrude as overtly sexual. In a BBC interview, Doron said that his production worked on the assumption that the king and queen enjoyed a "vigorous sexual relationship", both before and after the murder of Old Hamlet. How does this affect your view of the Queen, and of Hamlet's attitudes towards her?

- Branagh's 1996 film makes use of cut-away scenes and flashback. Through these flashback scenes, he is able to suggest that Hamlet and Ophelia were having a sexual relationship before the death of Hamlet's father, since we are shown the couple kissing and embracing in bed. There is no explicit evidence for this in the text; it is Branagh's interpretation of the play. How does this affect your view of the protagonist, his treatment of Ophelia, and Ophelia's madness?

- Both Olivier and Branagh make use of voiceover in their films. In both, Claudius is shown pouring poison into the ear of Hamlet's father, whilst the Ghost narrates over the top. This perhaps serves to validate the Ghost's claims; we are given visual proof that Claudius killed the king. Does this remove tension from the play? Does it affect your opinion of Hamlet, and his delay?

- Modern productions often look at the play through a feminist lens. Both Branagh and Doron's productions, for example, subtly draw our attention towards gender-based double standards. In Branagh's film, Polonius is shown dismissing a prostitute, before he reprimands Ophelia on being "most free and bounteous" in spending time with Hamlet. Similarly, in Doron's production, Laertes is shown to have a packet of condoms in his luggage after he lectures his sister on the importance of being chaste.

Key Themes

In this section, we'll discuss a few of the play's key themes. This is by no means an exhaustive list (there could never be any such thing!). Nonetheless, we'll discuss some important ideas, on which you could be asked a question.

Revenge and Hamlet's Delay

Consider the following questions....

"Shakespeare is deeply critical of vengeance. *Hamlet* suggests that revenge can only lead to ruin." To what extent do you agree with this view?

How far do you agree with the view that, "*Hamlet* is a traditional revenge tragedy"?

"In *Hamlet*, Shakespeare shows us that vengeance is not compatible with Christian sensibilities." Examine this view.

"Hamlet cannot execute his revenge because he has an Oedipus Complex." To what extent do you agree with this view?

How do Fortinbras and Laertes contribute to the theme of revenge?

As we discussed in the section on 'Addressing AO3', *Hamlet* is a <u>revenge tragedy</u>. Claudius, the **antagonist**, has committed an atrocity, and Hamlet, the **protagonist**, must avenge it. Such a description as this makes the play sound like a prototypical revenge tragedy, but, of course, Shakespeare diverges from tradition by creating a protagonist who is reluctant to fulfil his revenge; a hero who prevaricates over his assigned task, indulging in thought and reflection, instead of action.

Why does Hamlet delay?

In Act I scene v, the Ghost commands Hamlet to avenge him, and his son obediently and determinedly replies that, "with wings as swift as meditation or the thoughts of love", he will "sweep to [his] revenge." Of course, he does not; it takes the course of the entire play, in which he repeatedly meditates, prevaricates and delays, for Hamlet to execute his revenge. This procrastination bewilders Hamlet as much as it does his audience; he questions, desperately, why he delays his task when he has "cause and will and strength and means to do 't". For as long as the play has existed, critics have attempted to answer this question.

As we discussed on page 82, some post-Freudian critics use the Oedipus Complex to explain

Hamlet's delay. He cannot kill Claudius because he secretly wants to be Claudius; to murder him would be to attack his unconscious self. This interpretation, like the Oedipus Complex itself, is controversial.

The explanation offered by the Romantics is perhaps more popular. Romanticism, or the Romantic Era, was a movement in literature and the arts which, roughly speaking, began in England at the end of the 18th century and lasted until the mid-19th century. The movement championed the expression of emotion, feeling and passion, and emphasised the importance of individualism and sensitivity. For this reason, it is often considered to be a reaction to Age of Enlightenment, the intellectual movement which came before it, and which championed logic and rational thought. William Wordsworth, William Blake, Samuel Taylor Coleridge, John Keats and Lord Byron are all Romantic poets.

In keeping with these Romantic ideas and principles, Coleridge argued, in his *Notes and Lectures upon Shakespeare*, that Hamlet is unable to act upon his father's command as a result of his capacity for "enormous intellectual activity." Hamlet is unable to act, Coleridge suggests, because he is a deeply intelligent mind and sensitive soul, and having such powers makes one "a creature of mere meditation". As a result, he "loses his natural power of action." He becomes so lost in argument with himself, thinking and meditating, philosophising and rethinking, that it is impossible to come to a single conclusion and act upon it. The German critic August Wilhelm Schlegel lends weight to this idea, arguing that Hamlet "loses himself in labyrinths of thought" and is consequently unable to act.

"... if there be an overbalance in the contemplative faculty, man thereby becomes the creature of mere meditation, and loses his natural power of action [...]. [In *Hamlet*], we see a great, an almost enormous, intellectual activity, and a proportionate aversion to real action consequent upon it".

Samuel Taylor Coleridge

Remember: to achieve the highest AO5 marks, you must not simply refer to critics such as Coleridge or Schlegel. Instead, you must *assess* their views. If you agree with the Romantic argument, explain why, using evidence from the text. Similarly, if you disagree, explain why you hold this position, also using evidence from the text.

If you do object to Coleridge's argument, as well as the Oedipal reading of the play, then the question remains unanswered: why does Hamlet delay, and struggle to execute his revenge?

At the end of Act I scene v, in which the Ghost orders Hamlet to avenge him, the protagonist has already begun to lament the fact that this task has fallen upon him. He says:

"The time is out of joint. O cursed spite,
That ever I was born to set it right."

Act I scene v

This comment is perhaps more important than we might at first realise, and the possible answer to the question regarding the cause of Hamlet's delay. "The time is out of joint": Hamlet cannot avenge his father because revenge is no longer socially or morally acceptable, in Shakespeare's time. The Ghost belongs to a past age, based upon codes of martial honour and blood feuds, but Hamlet recognises that these codes are no longer appropriate.

The early seventeenth century was a time of social change. As Lucy Webster points out, "this is a society in the process of change, torn between past and present." There was a cultural shift away from medieval notions of honour to a more modern society, which no longer romanticised the vengeful spilling of blood, and sought to establish a safe and healthy national community. Such arguments can only be speculative, but perhaps Shakespeare realised that revenge and blood feuds – which were being glorified by the drama of his day – were destructive, harmful, and ultimately fruitless. Hamlet knows this too, and thus he struggles to complete his task.

This interpretation of the play suggests that the Ghost is a representative of a past age, who – in encouraging Hamlet to avenge him – is attempting to apply an archaic morality to a changed world. This idea is perhaps supported by the fact that the Ghost subscribes to Catholic doctrine (he claims to suffer in the "sulphurous and tormenting flames" of Purgatory), when the majority of Shakespeare's audience would have been Protestants. Shakespeare implies that Hamlet, too, belongs to the Early Modern, post-Reformation world, since he has him attend the University of Wittenberg, the city in which Martin Luther nailed his ninety-five theses to a church building, sparking the Protestant Reformation. Father and son, therefore, are divided: they belong to different worlds, with different values. Hamlet wants to obey his father, but "the time is out of joint." The task the Ghost wants his son to perform is no longer appropriate or acceptable.

Shakespeare may also have used costume in order to suggest that the Ghost is a relic from the past. Barbara Bleiman suggests that the actor playing this part would have worn "clothes of war that hark back to the battles of thirty years ago."

This interpretation of the play leads to further questions regarding revenge and vengeance. Notably, if Shakespeare is suggesting that the Ghost's command is based on archaic, outdated ethics which are no longer appropriate, is he criticising revenge? Is Hamlet wrong to murder Claudius, in the end?

Is Shakespeare critical of vengeance?

As we have already discussed, the protagonists in conventional revenge tragedies actively and eagerly fulfil the role of the avenger. They are horrified by the crimes committed by the **antagonist**, and relish the opportunity to take justice into their own hands. Shakespeare refuses to conform to this tradition, and instead creates a melancholy, inactive figure who bitterly laments the fact that he must avenge his murdered father: "O cursed spite, that ever I was born to set it right."

However, there are other characters in this play who *do* resemble the more conventional revenge tragedy protagonist: Fortinbras and Laertes. These characters serve as **foils** to Hamlet. As A. C. Bradley points out, we are meant to recognise the "parallelism in situation" between them: all three are the sons of murdered fathers, who feel duty-bound to avenge them.

"Laertes and Fortinbras [...] are evidently designed to throw the character of the hero into relief. Even in the situations there is a curious parallelism; for Fortinbras, like Hamlet, is the son of a king, lately dead, and succeeded by his brother; and Laertes, like Hamlet, has a father slain, and feels bound to avenge him. And with this parallelism in situation there is a strong contrast in character; for both Fortinbras and Laertes possess in abundance the very quality which the hero seems to lack, so that, as we read, we are tempted to exclaim that either of them would have accomplished Hamlet's task in a day."

A. C. Bradley, *Shakespearean Tragedy*

As Bradley points out, there is a "strong contrast in character"' between Hamlet and his foils: Fortinbras and Laertes are eager to avenge their fathers. The former sends "twenty thousand men" to Poland in order to capture a "patch of ground" which is of little value: it "hath in it no profit but the name". This clearly shows us that Fortinbras is capable of taking action in a way that Hamlet is not.

Similarly, Laertes shows that he is capable of action in his eagerness to avenge his father, Polonius. Indeed, his desire for vengeance is so great that he makes the deeply sacrilegious declaration that he will "cut" Hamlet's throat "i'th'church". This kind of blood-thirsty rhetoric is typical of a protagonist from a conventional revenge tragedy. Laertes' eagerness to take action, therefore, clearly serves as an ironic parallel to Hamlet's passivity.

"...let him come;
It warms the very sickness in my heart,
That I shall live and tell him to his teeth,
'Thus didst thou.'"

Laertes,
Act IV scene vii

The important question, however, is this: which character does Shakespeare approve of? Is he celebrating Fortinbras and Laertes' strong sense of honour, and holding them up to us as examples to be followed? Or is he, in fact, critical of them?

Let's focus on Fortinbras, Hamlet's Norwegian counterpart. Have a read of Hamlet's **soliloquy** in Act IV scene iv, beginning, "How all occasions do inform against me..." (perhaps watch it being performed by looking for it on YouTube).

This soliloquy comes after Hamlet has just seen Fortinbras' soldiers, and heard that he is marching to Poland. The Norwegian prince does not have much to gain from this mission; as the Captain tells Hamlet, the land that Fortinbras seeks to capture has "in it no profit but the name".

Hamlet's soliloquy appears to express admiration for Fortinbras. He appears to be in awe of "this army of such mass and charge", and praises the prince's "divine ambition". Reflecting on Fortinbras' actions in this way also makes Hamlet self-reflective and self-deprecating: he reprimands himself for "let[ting] all sleep" when he has "a father killed, a mother stained, Excitements of my reason and my blood". If one fails to follow Fortinbras' example, and instead behaves like Hamlet, inactive and passive ("his chief good and market of his time be but to sleep and feed"), he is,

Hamlet remarks, "a beast, no more." This suggests that Shakespeare is indeed holding Fortinbras up as an example to follow, and condemning Hamlet's inactivity.

This soliloquy, however, is more ambiguous than this: it contains subtle hints that Hamlet is not convinced by his own comments. He refers to Fortinbras, for example, as a "delicate and tender prince". Is this a fitting description? Is there perhaps an element of sarcasm here?

Similarly, though Fortinbras is courageous enough to "dare danger", he does so for the sake of an "egg-shell", and finds "quarrel in a straw". A "straw" and an "egg-shell" are both worthless objects, which suggests that the Norwegian prince is going to this monumental effort and risk for nothing.

Finally, the soliloquy ends with an emphasis on the death and the destruction that Fortinbras' actions will inevitably cause. His army "go to their graves like beds, fight for a plot whereon the numbers cannot try the cause". The "imminent death of twenty thousand men", in other words, will not achieve anything. Notably, the protagonist claims that Fortinbras is acting upon a "fantasy and trick of fame". Hamlet does not truly believe, therefore, that this mission will result in honour and glory for the Norwegian prince; rather, such a belief is a "fantasy" - illusionary. The only real consequences of his actions are death and suffering.

This surely suggests that Fortinbras is not being praised – at least, certainly not without qualification.

Nonetheless, it is Hamlet's inability to act which leads to the fall of Elsinore. Had he murdered Claudius earlier in the play, the lives of Gertrude, Ophelia, Polonius, Rosencrantz and Guildenstern might have been spared. Instead, he prevaricates and delays, creating more chaos and disorder in the court, until the tension that has persisted for so long is released in the final scene of the play, and the entire Danish royal family is killed. If Shakespeare is criticising those who act as Fortinbras does, and supporting those who philosophise as Hamlet does, this is a strange way of doing so.

Perhaps we must accept that the play is simply more complex and nuanced than this. Neither Hamlet nor Fortinbras are being held up as paragons to be emulated. Rather, the different courses of action that they take are both shown to be dangerous: Fortinbras' rash, mindless blood-lust has the potential to lead to pointless waste and pain, whilst Hamlet's endless philosophising ultimately paralyses him, preventing him from taking action until it is too late – which also leads to waste and pain. Ultimately, perhaps the idea that Shakespeare is trying to convey here is that we ought to achieve a kind of balance between these two extremes.

Is order restored at the end of the play?

In a conventional revenge tragedy, a sense of order and stability is restored after the avenger has fulfilled his mission. Is this true of *Hamlet*?

On the one hand, it is possible to suggest that the play's final scene is a reassuring one. As an outsider, Fortinbras is unpolluted by the corruption of the Danish court, and thus, by becoming the new Danish king, there is perhaps hope for renewal and recovery in Elsinore. Furthermore, the fact that he is appointed to the throne by Hamlet ("I do prophesy the election lights on Fortinbras, he has my dying voice") legitimises Fortinbras' rise to the Danish throne, and prevents his succession from appearing like a military invasion. This is further reinforced by the fact that Fortinbras shows respect for the Danish royal family: he says that Hamlet would have "proved most royal" had he had the opportunity to be king, and orders his men to carry Hamlet's body "like a soldier to the stage". The humble and respectful way in which Fortinbras conducts himself as he accepts his new position, therefore, is perhaps intended to inspire hope for the future.

An alternative reading, however, might suggest that the play's conclusion is in fact an ominous one, and that it leaves us with a sense of impending disaster and tragedy. Whilst Shakespeare's plays normally conclude with a rhyming couplet, for example, note how the final two lines of this play do not rhyme. Rhyme provides a sense of reassurance and finality – but Shakespeare has deliberately avoided this. The final word, moreover, is "shoot", which clearly has unsettling martial connotations, indicative of violence.

Drawing in AO5:

Various productions have followed this interpretation, by having Fortinbras' troops turn on the Danish people. Kenneth Branagh's 1996 film production concludes with the image of Fortinbras' soldiers destroying a statue of Hamlet's father, and thus we are left with a sense of destruction and violence, rather than peace and order.

Indeed, perhaps what is most unsettling about this final scene is that Fortinbras' dialogue echoes that of Claudius. Take a look at the following passages:

Claudius: we with wisest sorrow think on him, Together with remembrance of ourselves [...].

Have we as 'twere a defeated joy,
With an auspicious and a dropping eye,
With mirth in funeral and with dirge in marriage,
In equal scale weighing delight and dole...

Act 1 scene ii

Fortinbras: For me, with sorrow I embrace my fortune.
I have some rights of memory in this kingdom,
Which now to claim my vantage doth invite me.

Act V scene ii

Interestingly, both Claudius and Fortinbras use similar rhetoric in their acceptance of the throne. They both emphasise the juxtaposition between their "sorrow" at the death of their predecessor, and their delight in their own "fortune". Is this coincidental and inconsequential, or a clear attempt on Shakespeare's part to suggest that the Danish throne is now occupied by a second Claudius? If you find the latter argument the more convincing, then this clearly challenges the notion that order is restored at the end of this play: rather than entering a new era of hope and renewal, the Danish court risks repeating the past.

Your interpretation of the end of the play will affect your interpretation of the theme of revenge more generally. If order is restored, then vengeance appears to be a means of achieving peace. If not, then vengeance is futile, and only leads to further suffering and waste.

Kingship and Corruption

Consider the following questions....

"Shakespeare presents Claudius as a reprehensible, immoral and corrupt king, whilst simultaneously inviting us to sympathise with him." To what extent do you agree with this interpretation of *Hamlet*?

To what extent do you agree with the view that, in *Hamlet*, "every character is struggling to secure personal and political power for themselves?"

How far do you agree that, in *Hamlet*, "Shakespeare suggests that human beings are always corrupted by power"?

"Hamlet is gradually corrupted over the course of the play." To what extent do you agree?

"Though he is a villain, Claudius is a more effective king than Hamlet could have been." How far do you agree?

> <u>Something to consider:</u>
>
> Is Claudius an effective king?

Claudius is a murderer, a villain, and the antagonist of this play – but a case can be made for his being an effective ruler. In Act I scene ii, for example, he successfully handles the threat from Norway through skilful diplomacy: he sends ambassadors to "business" with the Norwegian king, Fortinbras' uncle.

In addition, Claudius is an articulate and persuasive public speaker. He cleverly acknowledges the tragedy of his brother's death (which prevents him from appearing callous and cruel), whilst simultaneously encouraging his people to be pragmatic and progress from their sorrow: 'we with wisest sorrow think on him, together with remembrance of ourselves'.

Similarly, notice how Claudius attempts to unite the court under his rule. **Inclusive pronouns** ("to bear our hearts in grief", "our whole kingdom") are used to project an air of solidarity – albeit this use of the 'majestic plural' is typical of a monarch. He then tells his courtiers that they "have freely gone with this affair along", with the "affair" here referring to his marriage to Gertrude. Thus, he is cultivating the impression that everyone is supportive of his rule and his decisions, which serves to legitimise his power.

In the same speech, Claudius discusses the military threat posed by Fortinbras, the nephew of the king of Norway. Again, he tackles this issue with language: Claudius repeatedly attaches the **epithet** "young" to the Norwegian prince, in order to diminish the threat he poses and project a sense of confidence. In doing so, he is able to manipulate the public mood and boost morale – a key quality for effective leadership.

Drawing in AO5:

"[Claudius] is not without respectable qualities. As a king he is courteous and never undignified; he performs his ceremonial duties efficiently; and he takes good care of the national interests."

A. C. Bradley, *Shakespearean Tragedy*

When Laertes enters the castle, with a mob behind him, to confront the king, Claudius calmly and skilfully placates him, through such means as flattery: "you speak like [...] a true gentleman".

Nonetheless, despite all of these virtues, Claudius' throne was wrongfully and immorally acquired. He is a murderer, who "from a shelf the precious diadem stole".

Does this prevent him from being an effective king? According to Italian political theorist Niccolo Machiavelli, it is perfectly possible for a ruler to participate in immoral activities and succeed as a leader. As we discussed on page 56, Machiavelli argued, in his work *The Prince*, that a successful nation requires a strong leader who can ensure the safety and prosperity of his people, and that it is acceptable to employ "some criminal or nefarious method" to achieve these aims. Thus, this ideology has the potential to redeem Claudius: the murder of Old Hamlet is acceptable if the country prospers under Claudius after this murder.

The issue with this argument, however, is that it is not clear that the country does prosper under Claudius. In fact, it appears to deteriorate.

Whilst Machiavelli's *The Prince* suggests that it is perfectly possible to be an immoral villain and a successful ruler at the same time, other theories that were circulating in Shakespeare's day argued otherwise. As we discussed on page 50, the medieval theory of microcosm and macrocosm (which was still influential in Shakespeare's time) held that a monarch's physical and emotional state was representative of the country as a whole; the king was the metaphorical "head" of the state's "body". This idea is often alluded to in *Hamlet*: images of the Danish nation and the human body, for example, in the description of Claudius' poison "cours[ing] through the natural gates and alleys" of Old Hamlet's body. This image implies that Claudius, in poisoning his brother, has also poisoned Denmark itself, and he does indeed cause damage to the nation by placing himself (a corrupt villain) at its "head", since this pollutes its "body" as well. Shakespeare employs imagery of disease and pollution throughout the play in order to underline this idea: Hamlet compares the air to a "foul and pestilent congregation of vapours"; Claudius likens Hamlet to a "foul disease" which must be treated carefully, whilst Marcellus recognises that there is "something rotten in the state of Denmark". Even Claudius himself acknowledges the corrupting effects of his crime: it is "rank" and "smells to heaven". This suggests, therefore, that it is impossible for Claudius to be an effective king, since the crime which elevated him to this position causes damage to the country that he is supposed to be governing.

Similarly, the idea that Claudius could ever be considered an effective king is also completely averse to the religious notions which dominated the Renaissance world. In killing his brother and placing himself on the throne, Claudius violates the concept of the "divine right of kings" (see page 71). Claudius' appointment to the throne was not decided upon by an act of God, but through his own action. Moreover, Claudius is unable to repent for his crime (since he cannot resign his "crown", "ambition", or "queen"), which ultimately serves to divide him from God: "words without thoughts never to heaven go". After the Protestant Reformation in England, the monarch became the head of the Church of

Drawing in AO3:

Notice how contextual details (the "divine right of kings", the Protestant Reformation etc.) are being drawn into the analysis here, and being used to further the literary discussion. Always ensure that you are relating context to your understanding of the play in this way; your work must never become a history essay!

England. Thus, for Shakespeare's contemporary audience, it would have been deemed deeply dangerous for a ruler to be as sacrilegiously divided from God as Claudius is.

Therefore, it is perhaps fair to suggest that, though Claudius has many qualities which are necessary for effective kingship (notably, his oratorical and diplomatic skills), these ultimately fail to redeem him of his crime. Importantly, moreover, these qualities fail to protect Elsinore in the end: in the final chaotic scene, Denmark is lost to Fortinbras. This could be considered the

inevitable consequence of a revenge plot which
Claudius himself sets in motion by murdering his
brother. Perhaps this is Shakespeare's way of
undermining the Machiavellian ideology: Claudius
cannot be a king in spite of his act of villainy, because
his very villainy destroys his country in the end.

Another Question:

Would Hamlet have made a good king?

If we can't find an example of good kingship in king
Claudius himself, can we glimpse it elsewhere? In the
final scene of the play, Fortinbras claims that, had
Hamlet had the opportunity to be king, he would have
"proved most royal". Is he right to say so? Is the tragedy
of *Hamlet*, ultimately, that a noble prince - who would
have made an excellent ruler - was never able to fulfil
this potential?

Hamlet's inaction is clearly one of the most
obvious arguments to make against this reading of the
play. As we mentioned in the previous discussion,
Claudius proves himself to be capable of taking decisive
action to protect the state in his handling of Fortinbras.
Hamlet, meanwhile, is unable to take action. He curses
the fact that he was "born to set [...] right" the injustice

done to his father, and repeatedly dismisses opportunities to execute his revenge - such as when Claudius is attempting to pray, for example. This inaction suggests that Hamlet would have been ineffective when it came to responding to military threats and protecting the state.

An alternative interpretation, however, might suggest that Hamlet's inaction is in fact a quality which is necessary for effective kingship. It demonstrates that he is able to evaluate, carefully, the correct course of action to take, as opposed to being "passion's slave" and acting impulsively, as Fortinbras and Laertes do. Shakespeare presents Hamlet as being capable of thinking before he acts, and the concerns which delay his action are serious and deserve such careful evaluation.

He is wary, for example, of his father's ghost being a "goblin damn'd", meaning an evil spirit. This is not a foolish superstition: in the seventeenth century, evil spirits were regarded as a genuine threat, capable of corrupting human beings. Thus, it seems likely that Shakespeare's contemporary audience would have considered Hamlet's wariness of this possibility a positive quality (indeed, James I, author of *Daemonologie*, showed a similar wariness – see page 66). Through such means as his "Mouse-Trap", therefore, Hamlet is, arguably, demonstrating an ability to evaluate the situation at hand, which is surely suitable in an effective king.

However, this interpretation is belied by Hamlet's character: his propensity for extreme emotion demonstrates that he is indeed "passion's slave", regardless of whether or not this galvanises him into taking revenge. Moreover, he does not always evaluate the right course of action in this way: in "the closet scene", he impulsively stabs and kills Polonius. This suggests, therefore, that Hamlet's inaction is not the product of careful evaluation and strategy, but rather, as A. C. Bradley puts it, "an unconscious fiction, an excuse for delay – and its continuance". Therefore, Hamlet's unreliable and erratic behaviour, coupled with his slowness to act, suggests that he would not have made an effective ruler.

Women

Consider the following questions….

'The female characters are entirely powerless.' To what extent do you agree with this interpretation of *Hamlet*?

To what extent do you agree with A. C. Bradley's view that, whilst Gertrude is "not a bad-hearted woman", she is "very dull and shallow"?

How far do you agree that, 'the depiction of women in *Hamlet* is deeply misogynistic'?

'In Ophelia, Shakespeare wants us to see a female parallel of Hamlet.' To what extent do you agree?

'The female characters are merely tools, used and exploited by the male characters to further their own ends. They are not presented as characters in themselves, with desires, thoughts and feelings of their own.' To what extent is this true of *Hamlet*?

In any discussion of women in this play, be wary of being **anachronistic**. Whilst Shakespeare's world shares many similarities with our own, the Jacobean way of life is also incredibly foreign to us. In particular, be careful when using such terms as 'feminist' or 'feminism', since the feminist movement did not exist in the 17th century, and thus such ideas simply do not apply to the play.

Similarly, be careful of making sweeping generalisations about life in Jacobean England, such as "women had no power". Different women led different lives; it is gross generalisation to group the entire sex together in this way. Though women, in general, wielded less authority than men, high-status women such as Gertrude and Ophelia had considerably more power than working-class women.

Something to consider:

How powerful are the women in *Hamlet*?

There are only two female characters in *Hamlet*: Gertrude and Ophelia. They are significantly outnumbered – and this itself is perhaps indicative of the amount of power that they wield in the play.

Indeed, even Ophelia's name indicates her powerlessness: it is derived from the Greek word 'ophelos', which means 'help'. In Act I scene iii, moreover, it is made clear that she is subordinate to Polonius, her father: the scene ends with her promising to refrain from meeting with and talking to Hamlet ("I shall obey, my lord"). Polonius undermines and belittles his daughter's emotions: "Affection? Pooh, you speak like a green girl unsifted in such perilous circumstance". When she tells him that Hamlet has "of late made many tenders of his affection for me", he turns this into a financial metaphor – "you have ta'en these tenders for true pay which are not sterling" – and in doing so he cheapens her feelings.

Indeed, a **lexical field** of commerce and transaction persists throughout this interchange between Polonius and Ophelia: "investments", "brokers", "sterling", "tender". This seems to reinforce the notion that Ophelia herself is a commodity, possessed by her father. Hamlet later puns on this idea when he calls Polonius a "fishmonger", which – though it could be interpreted as being humorously and harmlessly nonsensical – could also be seen as a pun on 'fleshmonger', meaning a brothel-keeper.

Gertrude clearly wields more power than Ophelia. This is indicated by the series of imperative verbs that she issues in Act I scene ii: "cast", "let", "look", "seek". However, this is, ultimately, the consequence of her position as queen, which in turn is the product of her marriage to Claudius. This suggests, therefore, that Gertrude's power – akin to that of Ophelia – emanates from her eligibility for marriage. The power of these women, therefore, is clearly limited. However, some interesting arguments can be made to suggest that these women grasp power through subtle and subversive means.

Another question:

How do Gertrude and Ophelia subversively empower themselves?

Ophelia's madness is perhaps an indication of her powerlessness. Indeed, feminist critic Patricia Barnard suggests that Hamlet impregnated Ophelia, and – finding herself helpless in the face of the cruel, gender-based double standards of the time – this left her with no other option but to retreat into madness and commit suicide. There is no direct evidence for this in the play; indeed, there it is never explicitly said that Hamlet and Ophelia had a sexual relationship at all – merely that he made "many tenders of his affection" for her, sending her letters. Nonetheless, Barnard suggests that, though it is never said, we are meant to understand that a sexual relationship has occurred between the two characters, and that pregnancy is the cause of Ophelia's madness. It is the unsaid subtext, articulated to us by subtle clues.

One such clue, perhaps, is Ophelia's seemingly nonsensical dialogue in Act IV scene v, after she has lost her mind:

"Tomorrow is Saint Valentine's day,

All in the morning betime,

Ans I a maid at your window,

To be your Valentine.

Then up he rose, and donned his clothes,

And dupped the chamber door,

Let in the maid, that out a maid,

Never departed more. [....]

Quoth she, before you tumbled me,

You promised me to wed.

He answers,

So would I 'a done by yonder sun,

An thou hadst not come to my bed."

Act IV scene v

In her madness, Ophelia sings a story about a girl who loses her virginity ("the chamber door let in the maid, that out a maid, never departed more") to a man who has promised to marry her, but she is rejected by him after they sleep together.

Thus, it is possible to suggest that Ophelia is singing of her own experience here: she is the girl, rejected by prince Hamlet. Shakespeare uses the song as a kind of riddle, which, once interpreted, shows us the reason for Ophelia's madness: she has been rejected and is ruined.

Drawing in AO5:

"The loving Ophelia, a 'ministering angel', dies chanting as an image less of victimisation than of the power of Shakespeare's language to evoke a unique beauty."

Harold Bloom,
Hamlet: Poem Unlimited (2003)

Alternatively, it is also possible that this song is merely intended to be a nonsensical product of Ophelia's insanity. Its vulgarity ("you tumbled me") is uncharacteristic of Ophelia, and Shakespeare perhaps only intends to use it to show us how utterly her madness has altered her. Ultimately, there's no definitive answer: the extent and nature of the relationship between Ophelia and Hamlet is ambiguous. It's your job to interpret it how you wish, supporting your answer with evidence from the text.

The dialogue of the other characters certainly encourages us to believe that Ophelia's madness has left her powerless: Claudius, for example, remarks that – without her "fair judgement" – Ophelia is merely a "picture" or a "beast". Many productions also endorse this view of Ophelia as mentally unstable and therefore powerless, such as Kenneth Branagh's 1996 film, in which Ophelia is subjected to hydrotherapy in a straightjacket.

> **Drawing in AO3:**
>
> A contemporary, Renaissance audience may well have believed Ophelia to be suffering from 'erotomania'; a form of madness brought about by unrequited love and repressed sexual desire, which was often associated with women.

An alternative reading, however, might suggest that there is "method" in Ophelia's madness, just as there is in that of Hamlet, which perhaps serves to empower her. This interpretation suggests that Ophelia's madness is not real; it is an act, which enables her to behave in ways that would have been deemed inappropriate and unthinkable if she was believed to be sane.

In Act IV scene v, Ophelia offers different flowers to the other characters on stage: "there's fennel for  you, and columbines..." Again, it is possible to understand this as a random act indicative of, and prompted by, her mental instability. However, to do so would be to ignore the fact that the flowers which Ophelia distributes had meanings attached to them, which a Renaissance audience may well have recognised. There are no stage directions to indicate who should receive a certain flower, so this is open to interpretation. Columbines signified marital infidelity, so it is possible that these are handed to Gertrude. Through the guise of madness, therefore, Ophelia is able to issue judgement on her fellow characters. Previously, she had kept her opinions to herself ("I think nothing my lord"), and thus, through feigned madness, Ophelia is able to gain a power that had previously been denied to her. Though she certainly lacks the same degree of power as her male counterparts, she is perhaps not wholly helpless, since she is able to grasp some power through subversive means.

This argument, however, depends on Ophelia's madness being feigned, rather than real – and it is certainly possible to reject that premise. Which side do you come down on, and why?

Similarly, it is also possible to suggest that Ophelia obtains a degree of power for herself in death. Though Shakespeare is ambiguous on the exact nature of her death, several characters express their concerns that it was in fact an act of suicide. The doctor in Act V scene i, for example, argues that Ophelia ought to be "lodged" in "unsanctified ground", because "her death was doubtful": he fears that it was not an accident, but a conscious act of suicide.

Today, we recognise suicide as the tragedy that it is, but a Renaissance audience would likely have been less sympathetic: suicide was considered a religious and a criminal offence. Those accused of ending their own life could be put on trial posthumously for murder, and a guilty verdict would lead to the deceased's family having their property confiscated by the state. Gertrude clearly attempts to avoid this fate for Ophelia: when she reports her death, Gertrude claims that an "envious sliver broke" beneath Ophelia's feet. The **personification** here, therefore, serves to emphasise the idea that it was the "envious" branch that was responsible for Ophelia's death, rather than Ophelia herself.

Irrespective of contemporary views on suicide, however, Ophelia's death perhaps reveals that she did wield a little power over her life, if only to end it. This is more autonomy than Hamlet could command: in Act I scene ii, he claims, regretfully, that he is unable to commit an act of "self-slaughter", because the "Everlasting" has "fixed his canon" against it. Hamlet, therefore, appears bound by religious doctrine, whilst Ophelia is not. Though this is evidently a deeply tragic power, it is a power nonetheless – and one that the protagonist lacks.

Interestingly, the nature of Gertrude's death is similarly ambiguous. Akin to Ophelia, it could be interpreted as an act of suicide. Though many productions (such as Branagh's) present Gertrude's death as a tragic accident, Marguerite Tassi notes that there is a "gap" of five syllables between Claudius' line ("Gertrude do not drink") and Gertrude's ("I will my lord. I pray you pardon me") in the rhythm of the dialogue. Perhaps Shakespeare intended this pause to indicate to the audience that Gertude is aware that the drink is poisoned, and is consciously deciding to drink it regardless, in order to spare her son. This interpretation is supported by the fact that Gertrude, whilst dying, is keen to alert Hamlet to the truth:

'No, no, the drink – the drink – o my dear Hamlet – The drink, the drink! I am poisoned.'

Act V scene ii

124

This reveals that the queen's ultimate allegiance lay with her son, rather than Claudius – and thus it is possible that she would sacrifice her own life in order to save him.

Alternatively, it could be argued that this five second gap in rhythm which Tassi notices is merely included to increase suspense before Gertrude drinks the poison, and that she is not, in fact, aware that it is poisoned at all. As with so much in this play, the matter is ambiguous; you must decide yourself.

The debate is relevant here, however, because, if Gertrude's death is a conscious, sacrificial act, she clearly wields some power over her own life, which challenges the notion that women are entirely powerless in this play.

Tragedy and Heroism

On page 63, we discussed Aristotle and his *Poetics*. A useful exercise would be to revisit this page and consider the extent to which *Hamlet* conforms to Aristotle's definition of tragedy. Is there a **peripeteia**, for example? Is there an **anagnorisis**?

This task is important because it is perfectly possible for you to be asked whether *Hamlet* is a tragedy, or what makes it a tragedy.

What makes *Hamlet* tragic?

When answering a question such as this, it is vital that you establish whose definition of "tragedy" you are working by. Is it Aristotle's? Can a play which doesn't meet Aristotle's criteria still be a tragedy? What is a tragedy? What does a play have to have in order to be one?

You might argue that structure is important, when it comes to defining and categorising a play. Based on his knowledge of Shakespearean and Classical drama, the nineteenth-century German playwright, Gustav Freytag, produced a diagram which examines the structure of drama. This diagram is known as Freytag's triangle, or Freytag's pyramid.

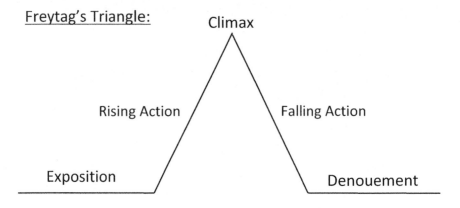

The **exposition** occurs at the beginning of the play. This is when the playwright provides the audience with important background information. It 'sets the story', situating the audience in the world of the play.

After this, action and intensity builds as the plot develops ("Rising Action"). This intensity reaches its high-point at the **climax** – the most intense and dramatic moment in the story. After this, the action and intensity of the story decreases, as conclusions are reached and issues are settled, until the story reaches the **denouement**. The denouement (which originates from a medieval French word meaning "unknotting"), concludes the plot and the subplots, "unknotting" all the questions and problems in the story, and ending the play.

Can we apply Freytag's triangle to *Hamlet*? Where is the climax? Is there a single one? Is there a satisfying denouement, or are questions left unanswered?

It should be remembered that Freytag's triangle does not only apply to tragedy, but to other types of drama as well. Indeed, this model could be applied to novels and short stories too. Perhaps, therefore - when it comes to attempting to define tragedy specifically, and assessing what it is that makes *Hamlet* tragic - we ought not to study structure, but character.

Is Hamlet a tragic hero?

It could be argued that Hamlet becomes increasingly heroic over the course of the play. He moves from a position of inaction and despair to once of confidence and conviction. He develops, in other words, into a decisive, active leader, who is capable of cleansing the "disease" from Denmark by avenging his father. Does this make him a tragic hero?

Hamlet's initial reticence is evident in Act I scene v, in which Hamlet first receives the Ghost's command to avenge his "foul and most unnatural murder": "O cursed spite, that ever I was born to set it right."

Shakespeare emphasises his reluctance here by adding a third line – "Nay come, let's go together" – to prevent the scene from concluding on a resounding rhyming couplet, which would convey a sense of certainty and conviction incompatible with Hamlet's state of mind. This, therefore, marks a clear contrast to Act IV scene iv, which concludes with the rhyming couplet, "from this time forth, let my thoughts be bloody, or be nothing worth." This rhyming couplet – which, unlike that mentioned above, does conclude the scene – is the traditional rhetoric of revenge tragedy. From this, it could perhaps be suggested that Hamlet develops into a Revenge Tragedy protagonist and a tragic hero.

However, as Hamlet develops into an active protagonist, his actions become increasingly cruel. Indeed, it could be suggested that – in becoming an effective leader – Hamlet shrinks further from Aristotle's model of a tragic hero, who suffers as a result of an "error of judgement" resulting from a character flaw (hamartia), rather than through "vice and depravity". Hamlet, meanwhile, is – arguably – guilty of these latter two attributes. As we mentioned on page 87, the Almeida Theatre's 2017 production of *Hamlet*, directed by Robert Icke, interpreted the central character in this way, by emphasising his potential for villainy. Following the murder of Polonius, Hamlet, whilst squeezing a bloody cloth, appears amused by the fear of Rosencrantz and Guildenstern as they ask where he has hidden the body.

Hamlet's killing of Rosencrantz and Guildenstern, moreover, also serves to indicate the protagonist's capacity for "vice and depravity". He never appears to express remorse for causing their deaths: "They are not near my conscience, their defeat does by their own insinuation grow." This crime is even more shocking when we consider that Hamlet does not truly know that his friends were conspiring with Claudius to bring about his murder; they may simply have been victims of the king's manipulation.

Similarly, Hamlet's "depravity" is also evident in the "closet scene", in which he stabs and murders Polonius. Though this "rash and bloody deed" was committed by mistake, Hamlet, akin to the deaths of Rosencrantz and Guildenstern, does not express remorse for it either. Instead, he condemns Polonius as a "wretched, rash, intruding fool". Towards the end of the scene, Hamlet states flippantly that he will "lug the guts" from the room; Shakespeare's use of language here is clearly intended to dehumanise Polonius in an impertinent way.

Whilst some productions attempt to maintain sympathy for Hamlet at this point by having him weep over the body of Polonius, there is, as A. C. Bradley points out, "no warrant in the text for the assertion".

"It is constantly asserted that Hamlet wept over the body of Polonius [...] but there is no warrant in the text for the assertion. It is based on some words of the Queen, in answer to the King's question, 'Where is he gone?':

'To draw apart the body he hath killed:
O'er whom his very madness, like some ore
Among a mineral of metals base,
Shows itself pure; he weeps for what is done.'

But the Queen, as was pointed out by Doering, is trying to screen her son. [...] His mother's statement, therefore, is almost certainly untrue [...]. Perhaps, however, he may have wept over Polonius's body afterwards? Well, in the next scene we see him alone with the body, and are therefore likely to witness his genuine feelings. And his first words are, 'Safely stowed'!"

A. C. Bradley, *Shakespearean Tragedy*

Hamlet, therefore, appears to fall short of Aristotle's definition of a tragic hero. He is not essentially good with a single a 'hamartia'; rather, he has many flaws, and he is, depending on your opinion, even guilty of "vice and depravity" – those negative qualities which Aristotle argued that no tragic hero could possess.

However, Aristotle's ideas about tragedy are not the only ideas out there, and you might perhaps take a more sympathetic and lenient view. The fact that the task of vengeance has fallen upon Hamlet is tragic: he does not want to perform it, he tries desperately to delay performing it, but familial obligations and outrage at his uncle force him into performing it. This comes at an enormous and tragic personal cost.

Perhaps a tragic hero is merely someone who must perform a difficult task, who suffers, and who we feel sympathy for. Do you sympathise with Hamlet? His acts of cruelty towards Rosencrantz, Guildenstern, Polonius and Ophelia certainly serve to shock and alienate the audience, but perhaps it should be noted that, even if our sympathy is lost during these moments of poor conduct, it is not necessarily irretrievable. It is likely, therefore, that we will come to sympathise with Hamlet at the end of the play, in spite of his former behaviour, when the revenge he has struggled so desperately to accomplish over the course of the play finally kills him.

Appearance versus Reality

"In *Hamlet*, Shakespeare suggests that placing one's trust in appearances is a fatal mistake which leads to disaster." To what extent do you agree with this view?

Consider the view that, "in his presentation of Hamlet's 'antic disposition', Shakespeare risks losing the audience's sympathy for his protagonist."

"The tragedy of *Hamlet* lies in the fact that nothing is truly real. Everything in the world of the play is an act, a façade or a delusion." How far do you agree?

How far do you agree with the view that, "a tension between words and deeds persists throughout this play"?

"The audience ought to be as suspicious of appearances as the characters. Hamlet is not always honest with us." To what extent do you agree with this view?

False appearances, facades, lies and deceit are everywhere in Denmark. The characters are always attempting to navigate their way through and round these false appearances in order to understand what is really going on.

> How is the relationship between appearances and reality presented in *Hamlet*?

In Act I scene ii, Hamlet stands apart from the Danish court. He looks downcast; he is wearing an "inky cloak", and he says little. However, when his mother reminds him that death is "common", and asks "why seems it so particular with thee?", the protagonist is suddenly enraged:

"Seems madam? Nay it is; I know not 'seems'.
'Tis not alone my inky cloak, good mother,
Nor customary suits of solemn black,
Nor windy suspiration of forced breath,
No, nor the fruitful river in the eye,
Nor the dejected haviour of the visage,
Together with all forms, moods, shapes of grief,
That can denote me truly. These indeed seem,
For they are actions that a man might play;
But I have that within which passes show –
These but the trappings and the suits of woe."

Act I scene ii

In this famous speech, Hamlet discusses the complex and paradoxical relationship between appearance and reality. The more he attempts to express his grief – by sighing ("windy suspiration of forced breath"), crying ("the fruitful river in the eye") or wearing mourning clothes ("customary suits of solemn black") – the more theatrical his emotions appear to be, "for they are the actions that a man might play.

Hamlet is deeply concerned by pretence and false appearances. Once he learns of his father's murder, he recognises how dangerous they can be: "That one may smile, and smile, and be a villain". Claudius' public image completely conceals his crime, and this causes Hamlet to suffer much frustration, resentment and fear.

Despite this, however, Hamlet also adopts disguises and hides behind false appearances in order to achieve his own aims. His "antic disposition" is an obvious example of this; he feigns madness. On page 122, we discussed an interpretation of the play which suggests that Ophelia's madness is also feigned, and that she does so in order to grasp a little autonomy for herself. Under the guise of madness, she can say or do anything she likes. Madness gives Hamlet a similar freedom; are false appearances liberating, in this play?

The theme of appearance versus reality is further underlined by references to theatre and acting. The players tell a story from Virgil's *Aeneid*, in which Aeneas, the protagonist, tells the Carthaginian queen Dido about the fall of Troy ("One speech in it I chiefly loved, 'twas Aeneas' tale to Dido"). In this account of the city's destruction, Pyrrhus, the son of Achilles (who died during the Trojan war, when Paris fired an arrow at his heel), takes revenge for his father by murdering Priam, the king of Troy and Paris' father. Akin to Fortinbras and Laertes, therefore, Pyrrhus is another parallel to Hamlet: a son who has had his father killed, and who takes revenge on his behalf. Hamlet requests that the players tell this story; he is perhaps hoping that it will galvanise him into taking revenge himself.

He is shocked, however, when one of the players begins to weep for Hecuba, Priam's wife:

"Tears in his eyes, distraction in his aspect,
A broken voice, and his whole function suiting
With forms to his conceit – and all for nothing!
For Hecuba!
What's Hecuba to him, or he to Hecuba,
That he should weep for her? What would he do,
Had he the motive and the cue for passion
That I have?"

Act II scene ii

137

Here, the distinction between appearance and reality is once again being blurred. A fictional story is causing a man to feel real emotion and weep genuine tears, whilst Hamlet does not act even though he has cause to ("the motive and the cue for passion").

This theme of acting is further emphasised when Hamlet stages his "Mouse-Trap". Though the protagonist pretends to be merely staging *The Murder of Gonzago*, he is really attempting to "catch the conscience of the king"; he hopes that it will confirm that the Ghost's allegations are correct.

Players, plays within plays, acting and pretence is clearly a recurring theme in this play. This contributes towards the wider theme of appearance versus reality, but it also has a **metatheatrical** side-effect. By repeatedly referring to plays and acting, the audience is made more conscious of the fact that they themselves are watching a play, performed by actors. It could be claimed that *Hamlet* is self-conscious of its status as a play.

In addition to the Players and the "Mouse-Trap", this play is peppered with several, more subtle metatheatrical references. In Act II scene ii, for example, Hamlet describes the sky as a "majestical roof fretted with golden fire", perhaps in reference to the ceiling of the Globe Theatre, which was decorated with stars.

All this functions to heighten our awareness of the play's artificiality, which is perhaps appropriate for a play that is so deeply interested in the relationship between acting and authenticity. Indeed, performance and pretence are so abundant in Elsinore that the relationship between acting and reality becomes ambiguous, to the extent that it becomes difficult to distinguish between the two. Though Hamlet claims that he is consciously deciding to adopt an "antic disposition", for example, Shakespeare encourages us to question the extent to which his madness is a performance and the extent to which it is real. His dialogue is obsessively repetitious ("O villain, villain, smiling damned villain!") creating a sense of the manic and frantic, which is suggestive of genuine mental instability, which in turns suggests that his madness may not be simply a mere performance. The play, therefore, is deeply concerned with the ways in which pretence and performance interact with, and exist within, reality, and metatheatrical references serve to expand this question outside of the world of the play, encouraging us to question the relationship between our reality and the artificial drama, and the extent to which pretence and false appearances exist in the 'real' world outside the stage, as it does within the play.

Of course, when one is aware that the appearances of those around them cannot be trusted, they naturally become wary, suspicious and cautious. In the play, the consequence of this is frequent spying and constant surveillance.

139

Spying and Surveillance:

Appearances cannot be trusted in Elsinore, and the characters know this. As a result, they resort to spying and surveillance in order to uncover the truth behind deceitful appearances:

- Polonius orders Reynaldo to spy on Laertes whilst he is studying in Paris.

- In the "nunnery scene", Claudius and Polonius spy on Hamlet as he talks to Ophelia. Polonius instructs his daughter to "Read on this book", so that "show of such an exercise may colour your loneliness." They are ensuring that she *appears* innocent, therefore, in order to deceive him. As Polonius points out, "with devotion's visage and pious action we do sugar o'er the devil himself." This word – "visage" – becomes something of a motif in the play: pictures and paintings are often referred to in order to emphasise the theme of appearance versus reality.

- Rosencrantz and Guildenstern are invited to Elsinore in order to spy on Hamlet. This is consented to by Gertrude as well as Claudius: "I beseech you instantly to visit my too much changed son."

- Polonius insists on spying upon Hamlet and Gertrude in the "closet scene". This, of course, leads to his death.

Gertrude's willingness to have her son spied upon, coupled with Polonius' decision to have Laertes watched by Reynaldo, suggests that, in the "prison" of Denmark, even family relationships involve a degree of surveillance. Is trust entirely absent in this play?

Though many characters engage in spying throughout this play, Polonius does so the most. Indeed, Richard Vardy goes so far as to suggest that Polonius is an "apparatchik, a bureaucrat, an agent of the state", who is obsessed with the "power that secret knowledge bestows in Denmark." He argues that the traditional view of Polonius as a "tedious old fool", to borrow Hamlet's damning remark, is misguided: Polonius, Vardy suggests, is much more perceptive and cunning than he is often given credit for.

"Polonius – as Lord Chamberlain (the chief official of a royal household), as Claudius' right hand man, as chief spy – is instrumental to the seizure and control of power and is at the heart of the corrupt and oppressive state.

Polonius is introduced by Claudius in Act I scene ii. His political importance is quickly established:

'The head is not more native to the heart,
The hand more instrumental to the mouth,
Than is the throne of Denmark to [Polonius].'

That Polonius was instrumental in securing Claudius' tenuous and contested claim to the throne is here beyond doubt."

Richard Vardy, "Stewed in Corruption – Polonius and the Politics of Denmark", *Emagazine*

Many productions of *Hamlet* agree with Vardy's interpretation of the play, and show Polonius assisting Claudius in the murder of Old Hamlet. This is, however, never made explicit by the text; it is only potentially implied by quotations such as the one that Vardy cites, from Act I scene ii. It is perfectly possible to dispute this view, and argue that Polonius is ignorant of the fact that his new king is a murderer – but you must argue your case and support your view with evidence.

The emphasis placed on spying and surveillance in this play may have been influenced by the politics of Shakespeare's day. Elizabeth I had a network of spies, employed to intercept letters and capture possible dissenters. As Vardy points out, a contemporary audience may have associated Polonius with Francis Walsingham, the queen's infamous spymaster.

The idea that power is maintained through spying, however, is certainly not limited to the world of Shakespeare's day. The National Theatre's 2010 production of the play, directed by Nicholas Hytner, for example, emphasised the relevance of this theme in the modern world by embedding CCTV cameras into the set. These remained onstage throughout the production, in order to emphasise the oppressive and omnipresent nature of surveillance in Elsinore.

Approaching a Question

In the exam, you will be given only one question; there is no element of choice. Try not to let this worry you: sometimes, having only the one question can be a positive thing, because it prevents you from wasting time as you agonise over which question to choose.

It is natural to panic when you first read an exam question. It is important, therefore, that you calm yourself down by reading and rereading the question carefully, and jotting down a few of your initial responses. Usually, once ideas start to flow, you realise that the question is less challenging than you originally thought.

Read the question carefully:

Remember that there are both AO1 and AO5 marks available for addressing the question fully and consistently. It is crucial, therefore, that you do not overlook key words. Take the following example:

> "Spying, deceit and corruption are rife in Denmark. Everyone is hiding behind a façade, and no one can be trusted." In light of this statement, examine the characterisation of Polonius in *Hamlet*.

WJEC Eduqas usually include a statement or quotation in their questions (though not always). Under exam conditions, it would be easy to read this quotation and discuss Claudius' corruption and capacity for deceit, or the role of Rosencrantz and Guildenstern, or how even Gertrude and Ophelia become embroiled in the spying and surveillance that is omnipresent in Elsinore. This, however, would be irrelevant, because the question is asking candidates to examine <u>the characterisation of Polonius</u>. It is essential, therefore, that you **always read and reread <u>every part</u> of the question**; do not only read the quotation.

Silly mistakes happen in exams. To minimise the chances of you making them, take time to read the question fully. Ring round or underline the key words, and make sure that you haven't missed anything.

Address the question fully:

The previous section warns candidates against accidentally overlooking certain details in a question, but sometimes students do so deliberately. Consider the following example:

> Consider the view that, "In *Hamlet*, Shakespeare suggests that, although he is a villain, Claudius is a far more effective king than Hamlet would have been."

Whilst this question is only a sentence long, it is making multiple different assertions about the play:

- Claudius is an effective king.
- Hamlet would not have been as effective.
- Claudius is a villain.
- It is possible to be a villain and an effective king at the same time.

You might be tempted to respond to this question by writing an interesting essay on whether Claudius is an effective king or not: but this only addresses the first bullet point. In order to answer the question fully, make sure that you are engaging with every part of it.

Find the Grey Areas:

Exam questions can often be very one-sided, or black-and-white. One feature of A/A* level essays is that they tend to pick out and discuss the **nuances**, or 'grey areas', in a question.

Here is an example of a question that has been 'picked apart' in this way:

> This question is asking you about our sympathies for Hamlet, but, before it gets there, it is making a very significant assumption about the play: it takes the idea that Hamlet develops over its course for granted. It is perfectly possible to take issue with this, and suggest that he does not develop into an effective leader, before you go on to discuss whether we sympathise with him.

"Although <u>he develops</u> into an effective leader and a successful hero, the <u>audience</u> lose sympathy for Hamlet over the course of the play." To what extent do you agree with this view?

> Which audience? Always look out for questions which make vague, general comments about the view or reaction of the audience, because there is no single audience. Shakespeare's contemporaries viewing the play in the 17th century, for example, may have held very different views from a modern audience watching a 21st century interpretation of *Hamlet*. Making this distinction in your essay shows that you are focussing very closely on specific words in the question.

What exactly do we mean by "an effective leader and a successful hero"? Some kind of definition, or criteria, must be established before we can decide whether Hamlet can be regarded as one. Are we working by Machiavelli's understanding of an effective leader, for example, or Aristotle's ideas on the tragic hero?

"Although he develops into <u>an effective leader and a successful hero</u>, the audience <u>lose sympathy</u> for Hamlet <u>over the course of the play</u>." To what extent do you agree with this view?

The question gives us a time period: "over the course of the play." Do you think that Hamlet is undergoing a process of development from the very beginning of the play, as this phrase perhaps suggests? Some critics, for example, take the view that Hamlet undergoes a very rapid transformation between Acts 4 and 5, and it is possible to argue that he does not develop a great deal in Acts 1-4. Stating that he has developed "over the course of the play", therefore, is perhaps misleading – depending on your view.

You might agree with the idea that our sympathies are lost, but is it possible for them to be regained? Perhaps we are constantly in the process of losing but regaining our sympathy for Hamlet as we watch this play.

Breaking down a question in this way will help you to find different ideas to discuss in your essay, and will make your overall argument more insightful and sophisticated.

Try annotating the following questions:

How far do you agree with the view that, "Hamlet is nothing more than a cruel and self-absorbed coward."

"The audience are more likely to sympathise with Laertes than with Hamlet." To what extent do you agree with this view?

"Rosencrantz and Guildenstern are concerned friends, eager to help Hamlet, who they believe to be mad. The protagonist judges them incorrectly and his treatment of them is abominable." How far do you agree?

"Ultimately, the play suggests that human life is meaningless and not worth living." To what extent do you agree with this view?

Consider the view that, "Polonius is not a 'tedious old fool' but a dangerous villain."

"Though she is foolish, and ignorant of the fact that her actions have grave consequences, the audience ultimately sympathise with Gertrude." How far do you agree?

Consider the view that, in *Hamlet*, "Shakespeare utterly undermines the genre of the revenge tragedy. Revenge is shown to be dangerous and wasteful, and not something to be celebrated."

After you have broken down the question, which will hopefully provide you with a few ideas, you are ready to plan.

Essay Planning

Writing practice essays can be a laborious and time-consuming way to revise. Though it is essential that you write a few full essays (ideally, your teacher should be setting these regularly), writing essay plans is an excellent way to revise.

Please note that revision essay plans are not the same as 'real' essay plans, which you write in an exam. A revision essay plan is a condensed version of a full essay; here is an example below. **You will not have time to write an essay of this length in the real exam.**

> 'The female characters are entirely powerless.' To what extent do you agree with this interpretation of *Hamlet*?

Introduction:

The introduction ought to analyse the question, and introduce the main thrust of your argument. In this case, I will pick up on the word "entirely", and take issue with it. This essay will argue that, though the female characters in the play are certainly less powerful than their male counterparts, they are not "entirely" lacking in power.

Paragraph One: The Treatment of Women

- Gertrude and Ophelia = lack the same degree of power that is enjoyed by the male characters.
- AO3: Even Ophelia's name indicates her powerlessness. It is derived from the Greek word "ophelos", meaning "help".
- She is subordinate to Polonius. A lexical field of commerce and transaction ("tender", "investments", "sterling") = emphasises the fact that Ophelia is considered a commodity.
- Hamlet puns on this idea by calling Polonius a "fishmonger". Though it could be suggested that the protagonist is merely being humorously and harmlessly nonsensical here, it could also be argued (AO5 – both sides of the argument) that he is deliberately punning on "fleshmonger", a colloquial name for a brothel-keeper.
- Gertrude wields more power than Ophelia. This is indicated by the imperative verbs which she issues in Act I scene ii: "cast", "let", "look", "seek".
- But: this is because she is the queen, which is the consequence of her marriage to Claudius. Akin to Ophelia, Gertrude's power emanates from her eligibility for marriage.
- This is somewhat paradoxical. AO3: in Elizabethan/Jacobean England, marriage usually entailed a loss of power for women, because wives became subordinate to their husbands.
- Concluding point: Women are clearly less powerful than men in this play, but this does not necessarily mean that they are wholly or "entirely" powerless.

Paragraph Two: Ophelia's madness

- Ophelia's madness could be used as evidence to support the view that she is "entirely powerless", since it shows that she does not even have control over her own mind and sanity.
- AO5: Patricia Bernard argues that Hamlet impregnated Ophelia, and that this left her with no option but to retreat into madness and commit suicide.

  └──▶ There is no direct evidence for this in the text, but it is perhaps supported by the sexual references which dominate Ophelia's seemingly nonsensical dialogue ("the chamber door let in the maid that out a maid never departed more" etc.)

- AO3: a Renaissance audience may well have believed Ophelia to be suffering from "erotomania", a form of madness that was often associated with women, and was thought to be the product of unrequited love and repressed sexual desire.
- Claudius claims that, without her "fair judgement", Ophelia is merely a "picture" or a "beast" – reinforces the argument that she is powerless.
- Branagh's 1996 film (Ophelia is subjected to hydrotherapy in a straightjacket) adopts this view.
- <u>BUT</u> (alternative reading, AO5) – it could instead be suggested that Ophelia's madness is a pretence/there is "method" in it. She uses it to issue judgements on the other characters, through the distribution of symbolic flowers. The power to judge and express her opinions

was previously denied to her in the play ("I think nothing my lord").
- Concluding point: though Ophelia certainly lacks the same degree of power as the male characters, she is perhaps not wholly helpless, since she is able to grasp some power through subversive means (such as feigned madness).

Paragraph Three: Suicide

- Similarly, it could be suggested that the women of the play are able to grasp some power through suicide.
- Shakespeare is ambiguous on the exact nature of the deaths of Gertrude and Ophelia; both can be interpreted as conscious acts.
- AO3: In early modern England, suicide was a 'mortal sin' and a criminal offence. Those who committed it could be put on trial posthumously for murder, and a guilty verdict could lead to the state confiscating the goods of the deceased, leaving their family in poverty.
- Ophelia's suicide could be considered evidence of her wielding some autonomy over her life, if only to end it. This is more power than Hamlet had at the beginning of the play, when he desired "self-slaughter" but feared the consequences.
- AO5: Getrude's death could also be regarded as an act of suicide. Though many productions present it as a tragic accident (such as Branagh's), Marguerite Tassi notes that there is a "gap" of five syllables between Claudius' line ("Gertrude do not drink") and the queen's ("I will my lord. I pray you pardon me").

- This pause is perhaps intended to indicate to the audience that Gertrude is aware of the fact that the drink is poisoned, and is consciously deciding to act in order to spare her son.
- Concluding point: The fact that both female characters have to resort to suicide shows that they did not wield much power in life. Nonetheless, it also shows that they are not entirely powerless: they still have the power to choose and act, and, in Gertrude's case, to try and save those whom they love.

Conclusion:

- Both Gertrude and Ophelia clearly lack the same degree of power that is enjoyed by their male counterparts.
- But: they are not wholly or "entirely" without power. They employ subversive methods in order to achieve their aims, such as madness, or, perhaps more tragically, suicide.
- The fact that they have to resort to these options shows that they are not powerful, but it also shows that they are not "entirely" lacking in power.

This is a really worthwhile revision task, because it encourages you to focus on a particular question, and to consider how you can draw relevant AO5 and, particularly, AO3 material into the discussion. Notice that there are only three paragraphs in this essay, but they are long, detailed, and full of in-depth analysis. It is better, generally, to have a small number of detailed paragraphs than many underdeveloped ones. Depth, in other words, is always better than breadth.

Flick through this guide and have a look at the questions which open every chapter in the "Key Themes" section. Pick a few and write essay plans like the one above on blank sheets of paper. At first, use the play and your notes to include important quotations, critical material and context. When you are feeling more confident, try to write some plans without using the plays or your notes.

Clearly, you will not have time to write a detailed plan like this in the real exam. Instead, your plan will probably look something like this:

Paragraph One: the treatment of women. Ophelia is treated like a commodity by Polonius. Gertrude appears to have power, but only because she is married to Claudius.

Paragraph Two: Madness. If Ophelia's madness is real, then it demonstrates her powerlessness. However, it could be argued that there is "method" in it: she feigns it in order to gain some autonomy.

Paragraph Three: Suicide. Both Gertrude and Ophelia's deaths could be interpreted as suicide. This shows that they wield some power over their lives, if only a very little.

Writing a plan like this in the exam will help to keep you focussed on the question, and ensure that your essay shows evidence of organisation.

Writing short plans like this is another helpful revision task. Flick through this guide and find some more questions that you have not written an answer to yet, and simulate the first 5-10 minutes of an exam by picking apart the question and writing a plan like the one above.

Writing your Essay

There is no magic formula for writing a good essay, and you will know what works best for you. Nevertheless, here are some key points to steer you in the right direction:

- As we discussed on page 156, it is, in general, better to write a small number of well-developed paragraphs than many short paragraphs. Look at the sample essay on page 163: this has only four paragraphs, as well as an introduction and a conclusion, but they are detailed and well-developed.

- However, when you are writing your long paragraphs, be careful not to digress from the question. You must remain focussed; as previously mentioned, there are AO1 and AO5 marks available for answering the question. You cannot afford to neglect it.

- This also means that you cannot regurgitate pre-learned material which is irrelevant or only vaguely relevant - examiners will spot this a mile off. Only refer to points that you have written in practice essays if they are <u>wholly</u> and <u>entirely</u> relevant to the question.

- Remember that AO3 is worth 20 marks. It is crucial that you are frequently referring to context. It must, however, always be <u>relevant</u> and <u>useful</u> for argument. Do not digress away from the play in order to explore context, and do not allow your work to become a history essay.

- Whilst, again, there is no magic formula for a good essay, this structure might help you to start thinking about what to write and how to draw all of the different information together:

<u>"Although he is a villain, Claudius is also an effective king." How far do you agree with this interpretation of Hamlet?</u>

<u>First Sentence:</u> A point which is clearly focussed on and responding to the question.
<u>For example:</u> *The question suggests that Claudius can be a villain and an effective king at the same time. This, however, is not possible, because Claudius' villainy causes harm to Denmark.*

Then: Closer analysis (AO2) which is supported with contextual information (AO3).

For example: *The medieval theory of microcosm and macrocosm, which was still influential in Shakespeare's time, held that a monarch's physical and emotional state was representative of the entire country. The king was the "head", metaphorically, of the state's "body". This idea is frequently referenced in Hamlet: images of the human body and the body politic are conflated, for example, in the description of Claudius' poison "cours[ing] through the natural gates and alleys" of Old Hamlet's body. This image implies that Claudius has invaded Denmark itself by murdering its king, and he does indeed cause damage to the nation by placing himself, a corrupt villain, at its "head".*

Then: If it is useful and relevant, draw in AO5 material.

For example: *Alexander Crawford lends weight to this argument, by suggesting that there is "considerable evidence of a general corruption and weakening of the state under the example and influence of Claudius".*

Final Sentence: Conclude by reinforcing your initial point.

For example: *This suggests, therefore, that is fundamentally impossible to reconcile being a "villain" with being "an effective king". Claudius cannot be both, and so he must be the former.*

By following this structure, you can ensure that your paragraph is both focussed on the question and prioritising AO3, which is vital given that this assessment objective is worth 20 marks. Nonetheless, AO3 is combined with AO2 so that the essay does not risk digressing away from the play in its discussion of contextual material.

Please note that it is not essential to include AO5 in every single paragraph of your essay - though it must be in there somewhere, of course.

See the next page for a sample essay, which draws together all of the examined assessment objectives.

Sample Essay

Below is the question that we picked apart on pages 147 and 148, and an example of a high-level answer that has been written in response to it. A helpful exercise would be to highlight areas of the essay which clearly show AO2, AO3 and AO5 (AO1 is more difficult to pick out, as it is demonstrated by the overall tone of the piece, rather than by specific words or phrases), perhaps using a different colour for each assessment objective. Alternatively, you could act like an examiner by writing 'AO2', 'AO3' and 'AO5' in the margin when you identify it.

"Although he develops into an effective leader and a successful hero, the audience lose sympathy for Hamlet over the course of the play." To what extent do you agree with this view?

Over the course of the play, Hamlet develops into a decisive, active leader, capable of cleansing the "disease" from Denmark by avenging his father. Ostensibly, this seems to suggest that our sympathies grow, rather than decline, as Hamlet becomes increasingly heroic. Alternatively, however, it could be argued that, in becoming a competent leader, Hamlet's behaviour becomes increasingly cruel – as indicated by his treatment of Ophelia and Polonius, for example – which risks the loss of our sympathy. However, it should perhaps be noted that, contrary to the implications of the statement, there is no single audience; whilst a modern spectator may feel their sympathies challenged by Hamlet's conduct, this may not have been the case for a contemporary, Renaissance audience.

The greatest change in Hamlet's character trajectory is his gradual evolution from a position of inactive melancholy to his being capable of decisive action. This, therefore, serves to signal that he is slowly developing into a competent leader; in the Elizabethan/Jacobean era, military invasion was a persistent threat, and thus a monarch could not afford to be as passive as Hamlet is at the outset of the play. This initial reticence is evident in Act I scene v, in which Hamlet first receives the Ghost's command to avenge his "foul and most unnatural murder": "O cursed spite, that ever I was born to set it right." Shakespeare emphasises his reluctance here by adding a third line – "Nay come, let's go together" – in order to prevent the scene from concluding on a resounding rhyming couplet, which would convey a sense of certainty and conviction incompatible with Hamlet's state of mind. This, therefore, marks a clear contrast to Act IV scene iv, which concludes with the rhyming couplet, "from this time forth, my thoughts be bloody, or be nothing worth", in which the traditional rhetoric of the revenge tragedy – a popular genre in Shakespeare's time – is adopted. After this moment, moreover, Shakespeare never has Hamlet deliver another soliloquy, which perhaps highlights the fact that he has progressed from his obsession with words, and, in doing so, has developed into an effective, active leader.

This development perhaps also serves to gain our sympathy. As Hamlet becomes increasingly capable of executing his revenge, he draws closer to rescuing Denmark from its "rotten" state, and thus we sympathise with his cause. This sympathy may have been felt more strongly by a contemporary audience, as a result of the medieval theory of microcosm and macrocosm – still influential in Shakespeare's time – which held that a monarch's emotional and physical state was representative of the country as a whole; the king was the metaphorical "head" of the state's "body". Claudius' corruption, therefore, is serving to harm Denmark, and this idea is reinforced throughout the play by a motif of pollution and decay: "foul", "rotten", "pestilent", "disease". This, therefore, serves to cast Hamlet's role as avenger in a positive light: we understand why he has to remove Claudius from the Danish throne, and, as a result, our sympathy for him is maintained as he develops into an effective leader.

However, as Hamlet develops into a dynamic protagonist, his actions become increasingly cruel and violent, which perhaps risks the loss of our sympathy. Indeed, it could be argued that, in becoming an effective leader and a successful hero, Hamlet shrinks further from Aristotle's model of a tragic hero. According to Aristotle, a tragic hero suffers as a result of an "error of judgement", resulting from a character flaw ("hamartia"), rather than through "vice or depravity". Hamlet, meanwhile, is perhaps guilty of "depravity". This interpretation is supported by his behaviour in the "closet scene", in which he stabs and murders Polonius. Though this "rash and bloody deed" is committed by mistake, Hamlet is not remorseful for it. Instead, he condemns Polonius as a "wretched, rash, intruding fool", and tells Gertrude that he will "lug the guts" from the room, with Shakespeare's use of language here clearly intended to dehumanise Polonius in an impertinent way. Though some productions attempt to maintain sympathy for Hamlet at this point, by having him weep over Polonius' body, there is, as A. C. Bradley points out, "no warrant in the text for this assertion" – a fact which is made even more appalling when we consider that "this was Ophelia's father". Instead, his thoughts are all for himself; as soon as he has committed the murder, he diverts attention back to his own concerns: "a bloody deed, almost as bad, good mother, as kill a king, and marry with his brother". The rhyme here establishes an inappropriate lyrical tone, which suggests that Hamlet is ignorant of, or indifferent towards, the gravity of his actions. Though Hamlet becomes increasingly capable of taking active leadership, therefore, he also becomes increasingly capable of cruelty – and thus his development perhaps comes at the expense of our sympathy.

Alternatively, however, it could be suggested that, though Hamlet's behaviour may serve to appal a modern audience, a Renaissance audience may well have maintained their sympathy for the central character. This is because his acts of cruelty were perhaps justified by the ideas of the Italian political theorist Niccolo Machiavelli, who, in his work *The Prince*, suggests that a successful nation required a strong ruler who can ensure the safety and prosperity of his people, and that it was acceptable to employ some "criminal or nefarious method" to achieve these aims. Although *The Prince* was banned in Shakespeare's England, Machiavelli's ideas had wide currency. Thus, a Renaissance audience may have seen Hamlet's decision to send Rosencrantz and Guildenstern "to 't", for example, as justified, since this is ultimately a part of his plan to remove the "incestuous, murderous, damned Dane", who is making Denmark "rotten", from the throne. Similarly, though Hamlet's treatment of Ophelia may serve to challenge our sympathy for the central character today, this may not have been the case during the original performance of *Hamlet*, since feminist criticism is a modern phenomenon. Thus, whilst feminist critics might attract sympathy for Ophelia and deflect it from Hamlet (such as Patricia Barnard, who suggests that Hamlet impregnates and abandons Ophelia, which leads to her suicide), it seems unlikely that a contemporary audience would have viewed the play in this way. Indeed, even if a Renaissance audience did consider Barnard's interpretation (which is not, explicitly, supported by the text), it seems more likely, given the prejudices of the time, that they would have held Ophelia culpable for this, rather than Hamlet, and have reinforced Polonius' argument that she ought to be "somewhat scanter of [her] maiden presence". Thus, Shakespeare – being conscious of the sensibilities of his time – may not have considered himself to be risking sympathy for Hamlet as he charts his development into an effective leader.

To conclude, Hamlet remains a morally ambiguous character throughout the play, despite his development into a decisive, determined protagonist. Though we can sympathise with his mission, and the need to remove Claudius from the Danish throne, his acts of cruelty towards Rosencrantz, Guildenstern, Polonius and Ophelia serve to shock and alienate the audience. Ultimately – however – even if our sympathy is lost during these moments of poor conduct, it is not necessarily irretrievable. It is likely, therefore, that we will come to sympathise with Hamlet at the end of the play, in spite of his former behaviour, when the revenge he has struggled so desperately to accomplish over the course of the play finally kills him.

Good Points:

This essay is of a very high-standard because it is consistently focussed on the question and makes some very interesting points. The candidate clearly understands that AO3 is double-weighted, because context is frequently drawn into the discussion. Nonetheless, the essay is never at risk of becoming a history essay; context is always relevant, and used to further the literary argument being made. The candidate also addresses AO2 by analysing specific quotations from the play, such as the motif of pollution and decay ("micro-analysis"), as well as making analytical arguments about the play as a whole ("macro-analysis"). It is fluently written, with an academic style and register, and there is evidence of alternative interpretations.

To improve:

The candidate focusses greatly on Hamlet's development into an "effective leader", but there could perhaps have been greater discussion of whether he becomes a "successful hero". The candidate seems to assume that these are the same thing – are they? Picking up on these nuances and subtle differences is often the mark of a really excellent essay. Nevertheless, examiners understand that students are under time pressure, and the candidate has explored his/her points fully. It is better to have a few well-developed paragraphs than many under-developed ones, so perhaps the candidate has used the time allowed wisely in not addressing this.

Glossary

Allusion – a reference (*"He made an allusion to Shakespeare"*).

Anachronistic – attributing something to a period to which it does not belong. For example, it would be anachronistic to refer to John Webster as a feminist, because the feminist movement did not exist when Webster was alive.

Anagnorisis – a term used by Aristotle in his *Poetics* to refer to the point in a play at which a character makes a critical discovery (it is a 'moment of realisation').

Antagonist – The character who opposes, or is hostile towards, the main character (known as the protagonist).

Canon – in literary terms, the "canon" refers to a collection of works considered to be the most important or influential (*"Hamlet is a canonical play"*).

Catharsis – the process of expressing, and thus cleansing oneself of, emotions. Aristotle believed that catharsis was the purpose of tragedy: it causes us to feel pity and fear, which then cleanses us of these feelings.

Climax – The high-point in the action of a story; the most exciting or important moment.

Denouement – The end of a story, in which everything is explained and concluded (French for "unknotting").

Dialogue – a conversation between characters in a book, play or film.

Didactic – offering instruction or teaching ("the didactic play instructs its audience to be wary of flatterers").

Ellipsis – a series of dots (...), which are usually used in quotations to indicate that a section of the original text has been omitted.

Epithet – an adjective which is considered characteristic of a person and repeatedly attached to their name.

Eponymous – the person or character after whom the work is named. For example, Jane Eyre is the eponymous heroine of the novel *Jane Eyre*.

Exposition – the beginning of a story, novel or play in which the plot is established, explained and 'set up' for us.

Façade – a deceptive, or false, outward appearance (*"She concealed her resentment with a friendly façade"*).

Foil – a person, character or thing which contrasts with (and so emphasises the qualities of) another.

Foreshadow – to hint or indicate a future event (*"the storm foreshadowed the impending disaster"*).

Hamartia – a fatal flaw, which leads to the downfall of the tragic hero. The term was used by Aristotle in his *Poetics*.

Imperative Verb – verbs which issue a command (such as *"Sit"*, *"Listen"*, or *"Run!"*).

Inclusive Pronoun – "we", "us", "our", "ourselves". These pronouns often evoke a sense of affinity and commonality between the speaker and his/her audience.

Lexical Field – a collection of related words; for example, a lexical field of disease might be *"pestilent"*, *"sickly"*, *"rotten"*, and *"decay"*.

Madonna vs Whore Complex – The depiction of women in literature as, exclusively, either compassionate, pure, obedient virgins ("Madonnas") or sinful, licentious and untrustworthy prostitutes ("Whores").

Metaphor – a figure of speech compares a person or object with something it does not literally resemble in order to suggest similarities *("The city was a jungle"*, *"life is a roller coaster"*).

Metatheatre – a metatheatrical play is one which appears to be aware of its status as a play. It may well draw attention to the fact that it is a performance, artificially created by writers and actors. Showing an awareness of the presence of the audience, perhaps by addressing them directly, is a common way of doing this.

Motif – a symbol which recurs or is repeated in a text.

Nuance – a subtle difference or distinction.

Oxymoron – a phrase consisting of two contradictory words, such as *"bitter sweet"*, or *"deafening silence"*.

Peripeteia – a term used by Aristotle to refer to a turning point, or sudden reversal of fortune, in a tragedy.

Personification – a personified object is something that is not human, but which is given human qualities or characteristics; for example, "the trees shivered fearfully in the wind". It can also refer to a human character who is intended to represent an abstract quality (*"he is the personification of greed"*).

Protagonist – the leading, or main, character in a play or novel.

Simile – The comparison of one thing with something else, through the use of comparative words, such as "like" or "as" (*"as innocent as a child"*).

Soliloquy – a speech which reveals a character's internal thoughts, and is unheard by any other characters present on the stage.

Symbol – Something, such as an image or a word, which is used to represent something else.

Zeitgeist – the "spirit of the age"; the defining mood of a particular period of history, which is demonstrated by the ideas and beliefs of the time.

Was this guide useful?

Notable is a new company, so we really appreciate all the feedback and advice that we can get!

Tell us what you think by emailing us at admin@notableguides.co.uk, or contact us through social media:

@notableguides   @notable_guides

Looking for a private tutor? We are delighted to announce that Notable is now offering this service. Drop us an email using the address above if you're interested.

Notable
www.notableguides.co.uk

Printed in Great Britain
by Amazon

12084499R00102